THE KATA *and* BUNKAI *of* GOJU-RYU KARATE

THE KATA *and* BUNKAI *of* GOJU-RYU KARATE

The Essence of the Heishu and Kaishu Kata

GILES HOPKINS

BLUE SNAKE BOOKS
BERKELEY, CALIFORNIA

Published by Blue Snake Books,
an imprint of North Atlantic Books
Berkeley, California

Cover calligraphy by Sifu Liu Chang-I. Cover photograph by Martha Hopkins. Cover design by Howie Severson. Book design by Happenstance Type-O-Rama.

Printed in the United States of America

The Kata and Bunkai of Goju-ryu Karate: The Essence of the Heishu and Kaishu Kata is sponsored and published by North Atlantic Books, an educational nonprofit based in Berkeley, California, that collaborates with partners to develop cross-cultural perspectives, nurture holistic views of art, science, the humanities, and healing, and seed personal and global transformation by publishing work on the relationship of body, spirit, and nature.

North Atlantic Books' publications are distributed to the US trade and internationally by Penguin Random House Publishers Services. For further information, visit our website at www.northatlanticbooks.com.

PLEASE NOTE: The creators and publishers of this book disclaim any liabilities for loss in connection with following any of the practices, exercises, and advice contained herein. To reduce the chance of injury or any other harm, the reader should consult a professional before undertaking this or any other martial arts, movement, meditative arts, health, or exercise program. The instructions and advice printed in this book are not in any way intended as a substitute for medical, mental, or emotional counseling with a licensed physician or healthcare provider.

Library of Congress Cataloging-in-Publication Data

Names: Hopkins, Giles, author.
Title: The kata and bunkai of goju-ryu karate : the essence of the heishu and kaishu kata / Giles Hopkins.
Description: Berkeley, CA : North Atlantic Books, [2018] | Includes bibliographical references and index.
Identifiers: LCCN 2017028006 (print) | LCCN 2017049297 (ebook) | ISBN 9781623172008 (e-book) | ISBN 9781623171995 (pbk.)
Subjects: LCSH: Karate.
Classification: LCC GV1114.3 (ebook) | LCC GV1114.3 .H66 2018 (print) | DDC 796.815/3--dc23
LC record available at https://lccn.loc.gov/2017028006

3 4 5 6 7 8 9 KPC 24 23 22 21

To my teachers and fellow students.

CONTENTS

PREFACE

There is a pattern and structure to all things. Only we can't see it. Our job is to discover that pattern and structure and work within it, as part of it.
—RICHARD FLANAGAN, *THE NARROW ROAD TO THE DEEP NORTH*

SOMETHING ABOUT IT vaguely reminded me of an old Woolworth's lunch counter. There were two or three tables, covered in checkered vinyl, and a small counter with stools. Stout older women stood or sat behind the counter, watching a small television tuned to a sumo tournament. We had eaten here often in our first weeks in Okinawa and had come to refer to it as "Ni-kai." It was one of the first places Matayoshi sensei had taken us when we arrived. We followed him through the department store, past the butcher's aisle with its pigs' heads, past the kimonos and the perfumes, to the lunch counter on the second floor. Matayoshi sensei ordered green tea. A fly was buzzing around us, hovering over the teacups. Matayoshi sensei picked up a pair of *ohashi* from a container on the table—the cheap unfinished wooden chopsticks that come with take-out orders and that you have to pull apart. *Ah,* I thought, *I'm in Japan—the legend of Musashi, who could pick flies out of the air with chopsticks.* I'd seen the movie and read the book. This was Shinpo Matayoshi, the famous ancient weapons art *(kobudo)* master, a Living Treasure in Okinawa. But Matayoshi didn't take the chopsticks out of the wrapper. He hardly interrupted his conversation with my teacher, in fact, but as the fly briefly stopped its flight, coming to rest on the checkered vinyl tablecloth, he swatted it with the unwrapped *ohashi*. The fly was dead and swept off the table. Not the stuff of legends, but infinitely more practical.

ACKNOWLEDGMENTS

THE REASONS ONE PRACTICES any martial art may be idiosyncratic and varied, but the practice of martial arts owes much to others, and not just to one's teachers but to all of the people one has had occasion to train with because martial arts cannot be truly learned without others. I have learned a great deal from my teachers, most notably Kimo Wall, Gibo Seiki, and Matayoshi Shinpo, but also from Sifu Liu Chang I and a number of different Taiji teachers.

I have also gained valuable insight from my peers and fellow students, particularly Bill Diggle, long-time student and training partner, who also helped with the photographs for this book, and Ivan Siff, with whom much of this journey into an understanding of Goju-ryu kata began so many years ago.

I would also like to extend my thanks and appreciation to Michael DeMarco, publisher of the *Journal of Asian Martial Arts,* who encouraged me to write about the martial arts by publishing my early essays on Goju kata and bunkai, and the editors and production staff at North Atlantic Books for their kind help and assistance, especially Erin Wiegand, Louis Swaim, and Christopher Church.

And lastly, of course, I would like to sincerely thank my family, especially my wife Martha, for their patience and understanding.

INTRODUCTION: KATA AND BUNKAI

ON A HOT JULY EVENING IN 1986, I was standing in the dojo (martial arts training hall) listening to Matayoshi Shinpo explain one of the postures of Kakuho, a form (kata) from the Kingai-ryu system. We had been walking up and down the floor in crane stance, the toes of one foot curled under, ready to throw small pebbles or sand into an attacker's face, arms out to the side like wings. Matayoshi had come down earlier to watch *kobudo* training. When we had finished, we began training some of the empty-hand kata of Matayoshi's family system and our own Goju-ryu. It was already late in the evening. Sometimes Matayoshi would stop and try to explain something with the few English words he knew and then laugh.

"You no show," he would say. "OK?" That summer, sitting in an ice cream shop in downtown Naha, Matayoshi had heard a particularly strident American pop song. The singers' voices were harsh and nasal as they repeated the chorus, "Show me; show me." Matayoshi had asked what the words meant, and from then on, he used the words frequently, and laughed.

At the moment, however, he was trying to explain how one of the moves in the kata was used. Although the application seemed obvious, we couldn't figure out what he was trying to get across. With Matayoshi's peculiar collection of a few dozen English words or phrases and our handful of Japanese words, it was like some hilarious game of charades. Matayoshi would bend down and pretend to pull up clumps of imaginary grass (we later realized).

Then he would rear back with both arms up in front of his body, elbows in, forearms vertical, wrists bent so that the hands, held above the head, formed claws. Then he would stop and hold one hand up with index finger and thumb spread apart.

FIGURE A.1. Matayoshi demonstrating Kakuho

"You know?" he would ask. Of course we didn't.

Finally, someone went for a small pocket dictionary.

"*Mushi,*" Matayoshi said, pointing to the word *insect.*

"*Midori.*"

We all laughed. Matayoshi had only been trying to explain that it was a praying mantis technique. Nothing more. It made me wonder how many other things we had missed in translation that summer, and how situations not so different from this one may have affected the Okinawan martial arts in general. Were secrets lost in translation? What sorts of things had other students misunderstood along the way?

The history of Goju-ryu has been researched, second- and third-generation teachers have been interviewed, and each new journal article or book comes up with another theory about kata. Every teacher seems to have a new and different explanation of *bunkai* (the analysis of kata applications), and internet discussion groups abound with imaginative discoveries of kata's meaning and its applications. But how could so many practitioners be at odds about the meaning of things so fundamental to their art, to what they practice on a daily basis? Why don't we know what kata movements really mean?

Every school seems to have its claim, well-established through various lineages, to authenticity, to its own interpretation of the applications of kata. In the spirit of equanimity and brotherhood, students and teachers all seem to agree that there are many different ways to interpret kata—suggesting that there is not one "right" application for each move, but also that there are no wrong answers. But is it logical to suggest that kata is a collection of generic techniques so shorn of their original meanings as to be open to any and all interpretations? I find it hard to imagine that whoever made and formalized kata movements could have been so intentionally cryptic.

The sad thing is that given this state of confusion with kata, some have, lamentably, though I suppose understandably, thrown out the baby with the bath water and chosen to point an accusatory finger and shout, "The emperor has no clothes," exclaiming that the kata don't mean anything—the movements are just movements and there is no system to be understood. Or the obverse, that the movements can mean anything. How did we get to this point?

A few years ago, I happened on a translation of the minutes of the 1936 meeting of karate masters, government officials, and journalists in Patrick McCarthy's *Ancient Okinawan Martial Arts: Koryu Uchinadi*. The meeting was sponsored by the Ryukyu Newspaper Company, but its primary organizer was Nakasone Genwa. Though Mr. Nakasone went on to publish a number of books on karate, he seemed a curious figure to be so instrumental in this gathering of prominent martial artists. McCarthy notes that after graduating from college, Nakasone moved to Tokyo, became involved in the socialist movement there, and "served as the publisher of its newspaper."[1] It struck me then that this ancient tradition of martial arts—a tradition, it has been suggested, going back to Bodhidharma—was not immune to the pressures of politics and different social agendas. Perhaps I was naive to think there was anything that could survive the insidious influence of politics.

Many of us perhaps still naively believe that traditions—or the high-mindedness of certain larger-than-life individuals—may protect a practice from the social or political influences of the world in which it exists. There is, in some circles, the rather ingenuous notion that traditional arts are somehow independent of politics. But to suggest that any martial art, traditional or otherwise, can develop in a political vacuum is to say that

FIGURE A.2. In old Shuri

it exists outside of history. This is the same as arguing that Shakespeare or Mozart or Picasso are somehow independent of the historical events that in fact helped shape them. We are tempted to imagine that their work exists outside history because it seems transcendent, that it resonates today as much as it did with generations of sympathetic students of the arts in the past—but this is just not the case.

The underlying agenda of the 1936 meeting sponsored by the Ryukyu Newspaper Company was to find ways to popularize karate, make it more acceptable to the public, and give it a less violent image. In the process, there was a not-so-subtle attempt to make karate less Chinese, to Japanize karate. Perhaps adaptation and change are themselves part of the inexorable forces of history, but the danger is that in trimming the roots of the figurative bonsai tree, one may unintentionally kill the tree.

In his short essay *Karatedo Gaisetsu: An Outline of Karatedo,* which McCarthy dates March 23, 1934, it is evident that Miyagi Chojun was already thinking about the nature of karate and its popular perception by the time of the 1936 meeting. In this early essay, Miyagi emphasized that "training karate-do improves one's health" and that "physical and mental unity develops an indomitable spirit."[2] Certainly these were laudable goals and might even convince a wary public that the aim of true karate practice was in keeping with traditional Japanese values and would develop physical as well as spiritual strength in Japan's youth. At times in the minutes of the 1936 masters meeting, it would seem that there were disagreements—most notably over the place and importance of classical (of Chinese origin) kata—but it is clear that the participants were generally united in their efforts to popularize karate.

The larger question for Okinawan karate, of course, is whether there was any lasting effect on the development of karate in the twentieth century. We know at least that the name changed. According to the minutes of the 1936 meeting, Nakasone Genwa's first order of business was to recommend that the name of Okinawan karate be officially changed, using the kanji characters for "empty hand" (空手) instead of the characters for "Chinese hand" (唐手) as had been the tradition. Although there seems to be no real objection to this name change, some participants at the meeting pointed out that the general population recognized the term *toudi* (Chinese hand) or more simply *te* (hand). At least in part, it seemed to be a question of familiarity, what was recognizable. Others, however, pointed out that there were those—particularly in the school systems—who resented the term *tou*,[3] the name for the Tang dynasty used to mean China.

In this case, it seems fairly clear that this was a political issue—a change in tradition driven by the exigencies of contemporary politics. But, one might ask, what's in a name? As Miyagi sensei suggests, "Names change, like examples do; it depends upon the times,"[4] as if to imply that this would be a change in name only, having little other effect on the practice of karate or how it was taught. But which changes are acceptable because they are inconsequential, and which changes are unacceptable because their effect is detrimental over time?

The second order of business at the 1936 meeting, put forward by Vice Commander Fukushima Kitsuma of the regional military headquarters, was to recommend that new kata—Japanese kata with Japanese names— be created. Behind this suggestion, coming as it does from outside the circle of Okinawan karate masters, was the need to eradicate evidence of Chinese influence on Japanese culture. Ostensibly, of course, the discussion is again couched in terms that suggest a need to popularize Okinawan karate, which, as Nakasone Genwa suggests, "is in a slump these days."[5] However, in no uncertain terms, Miyagi says that "the classical kata must remain."[6] It is easy to understand why he was so insistent when one remembers the first precept of Goju-ryu put forward by Miyagi: *It should be known that secret principles of Goju-ryu exist in the kata—* and, of course, the kata he was referring to here are the classical kata of Chinese origin. So how does one reconcile these seemingly contradictory concerns? How do you popularize karate, making it less violent and more acceptable to the general public, and preserve the old kata—kata that are filled, for example, with neck-breaking techniques?

Karate had already become a part of the Okinawan school system as early as 1909.[7] Whatever the reasons for this move, I believe, it would have far-reaching consequences. A martial art practiced by schoolchildren is necessarily very different from the system of self-defense trained by the Okinawan warrior class *(bushikaikyu)* or the monk-warriors of China who may have developed the original kata. With Gekisai Dai Ichi and Gekisai Dai Ni—and various other "training" subjects added later by other teachers—Miyagi Chojun and others created "generic" kata that could more safely be taught to young people. A beginner's curriculum based on these training subjects—along with a healthy dose of *kihon* (fundamental) exercise—would be less lethal, and a teacher would not be giving away the art's "secrets."

This seems to have been a goal that many Okinawan karate masters shared: not intentionally to hide real karate, but to popularize a version that would be more acceptable to the public. Kata were preserved, but applications received less emphasis. Group exercise and physical conditioning replaced traditional application of technique because teachers considered the techniques too dangerous for schoolchildren.

FIGURE A.3. *Tsubo,* used as a training tool to strengthen the body, stacked in a back alley in Naha

This shift in emphasis, however, continued in the post–World War II years. Dan Smith, a longtime Shorin-ryu teacher, argues that the spread of karate to mainland Japan led to teachers who "did not stay with the Okinawans long enough to learn, and the karate that was taught in the beginning was *kihon*." The same thing affected karate in Okinawa after the war, Smith goes on to say, for a variety of reasons. The older teachers in Okinawa—those that knew the "secrets"—far from any intentional effort at hiding technique, Smith writes, were merely responding to "the changing times." Smith suggests that they "designed their instruction to meet the perceived needs of the day.... Emphasis was put on *kihon,* kata and *jiu kumite* [free sparring]."[8]

Others have not been so charitable. Anthony Marquez, writing in the now defunct *Bugeisha* magazine, argues that even second-generation Okinawan teachers didn't know the old applications. Marquez writes that Masanobu Shinjo sensei told him that the "old techniques died with the past generations."[9]

Whatever the case, forgotten or just not taught, kata, and by inference the interpretation of its applications, has become a kind of modern-day Gordian knot; no one seems to have the key to untangle its mysteries. Few seem able to agree on what it means or what it was originally meant to teach. Some have tried to reconcile their differences of interpretation by suggesting that kata contain an almost infinite variety of techniques, each technique open to multiple interpretations. Still others, armed with an arsenal of Japanese terms, describe kata as if it were an onion and the different applications of its techniques merely layers of hidden meaning.

Whether it is the intent of these teachers or not, the suggestion is that if my interpretation of a move in kata is different from yours, then we are just working on different levels. This sort of response, notwithstanding its unchallenged acceptance in many circles, may conceal more ignorance than understanding, revealing an incomplete knowledge of the system while fostering a general acceptance of anything that seems to work. And it is this that has led some karate practitioners, faced with these ambiguities and a host of creative explanations that often strain credulity, to abandon the notion that kata has anything to do with real fighting, or self-defense, or that we will ever be able to unravel its secrets.

And yet the practice of kata is an almost sacrosanct tradition in Okinawan karate dojos. Through endless hours of kata practice, students are told, "Every inch of movement has meaning." With this encouragement, the teacher only hopes that the student of karate will bring life to the kata. The difficulty comes with the student's understanding of this advice and how one learns karate, for the most part, through imitation and creative invention.

Most movement, particularly kata movement, is taught through imitation: monkey see, monkey do. There is little discussion or verbal instruction of kata, even in traditional schools. Toguchi Seikichi sensei, the head of Shoreikan Goju-ryu until his death in 1998, makes this clear in his description of training in the old days on Okinawa: "Both Higa and Miyagi were very strict, and questions were not permitted during training."[10]

Yagi Meitoku sensei, the senior student to have trained under both Miyagi and Higa, said that training in those days involved long hours of conditioning drills, and only after a number of years would Miyagi even begin to teach kata to a student. Few of Miyagi's students, Yagi says, learned anything more than the "beginner's way ... with no understanding of what they were learning." Yagi goes on to say that Master Miyagi "would very rarely give insights or meaning to the kata that he taught until the student showed mastery of the form through hard and consistent training," and few, according to Yagi, stayed long enough to learn anything beyond the rudiments of kata.[11]

This is still true in most traditional schools of Okinawan karate today. The beginning student simply stands in the back of the dojo and does his or her best to follow the other students. What little verbal instruction there may be is usually simple and rudimentary: posture, breathing, and stance, for example. Beyond this, of course, the beginning student needs a great deal of repetition. Anything more than this—a philosophical discussion of martial principles, for instance—would be lost on the beginner; he or she has no basis for understanding it. Additionally, one might also argue that this traditional model fits the teacher's natural wariness of beginners, who, for the most part, are not likely to stay long enough to learn what the teacher may really have to teach, to learn anything more than beginner's karate. In the process, the teacher does not give away the "secrets" (the applications, in this case) of the kata to students who aren't ready for them. A further rationale is that the movements must be thoroughly ingrained before one learns how to apply them, or the movements themselves will be compromised in an attempt to force their application. The teaching method provides a natural safeguard against either of these scenarios. At the same time, however, students are left with the impression that the kata is intentionally cryptic in order to foster the creative interpretation of martial techniques—that is, the applications.

FIGURE A.4. The author with his son Noah

Since the kata is learned through imitation, and the principles of movement in karate are generally not openly taught, one is left to discover meaning for oneself. Anthony Mirakian, a well-known Goju-ryu teacher and early pioneer in bringing Meibukan Goju-ryu to America, supports Toguchi's observation that "there was very little talking" in the traditional Okinawan dojo. Mirakian goes on to say that, "Generally, once a student was shown the kata, he was expected to correct the movements himself ... the applications were left to the student's imagination and inquisitiveness."[12]

The trouble is that this discovery method, while rich and imaginative—perhaps even personally rewarding—gives the impression that any interpretation of kata movement that seems to work is OK. In fact, this line of argument suggests there is no wrong or right, just different points of view. And this is the problem. When students learn kata solely through imitation—rather than in conjunction with a thorough discussion of the martial principles involved and illustrated in the kata—then the movements will be preserved, but their applications will most likely be misunderstood.

In his last book, on the "advanced techniques" of Goju-ryu karate, Toguchi, in effect, suggests that he developed his modern training kata to bridge this gap between kata and its applications. (These are the Shoreikan subjects Fukyu, Gekisai, Gekiha, and Kakuha.) Traditional methods of instruction—that is, imitation without asking any questions—did not satisfy the inquisitive nature of American GIs, and so Toguchi developed a series of basic katas and corresponding two-person drills *(kata bunkai)* to show applications. He did this, he says, because he "could not speak English" and he believed "a two-person sequence of the kata would give clear answers to the questions posed by the Americans."[13] However, these training subjects do not provide the keys to understand the movement and principles of the original classical kata of Chinese origin. This is particularly true of the two-person sequences that Toguchi developed—their techniques being elementary and the principles of Toguchi's two-person application drills misleading with their front-to-front straight-line movement. So, even though this did introduce a different methodology into the instruction of karate, it did nothing to explain the movement or techniques of the Goju-ryu classical subjects. The techniques and patterns are fundamentally different.

The problem, as Patrick McCarthy sees it, is that "the formula once used to interpret its [kata] application principles has all but vanished."[14] But the "formula" is not necessarily the problem. It is the methods we use to teach karate that have often obscured the message, and the methods have been passed on from teacher to student, maintaining a venerable tradition that in some quasi-religious sense is meant to test the character of the student through long hours of unquestioning repetition. The teacher's methods are not questioned; the teacher has attained his or her own exalted rank through the very means that he or she is using to guide the student. The same understanding will somehow be conveyed to the dedicated student—like a flash of Zen enlightenment—only after years of training. The kata becomes a kind of a koan for the karate student; he tests his understanding of the kata as he delves into more and more creative explanations for the applications of the individual moves.

This is the traditional approach to the study of kata. Yet the checks and balances that a thorough understanding of martial principles would provide no longer seem to exist. They have been eviscerated by rationalizations of multiple interpretations or the mystique of advanced levels of understanding. Or they have merely sunk under the burdensome weight and authority of different lineages. Certainly the discovery method is not without its benefits. It forces the student, Anthony Mirakian says, to become "highly observant, one of the most important factors in mastering karate."[15] The question is whether this benefit outweighs the drawbacks, considerable as they are, that have led to a general confusion about kata and its applications.

By all appearances, some traditionalists have gotten pretty good at coming up with creative interpretations of kata. There's a lot of stuff out there, even if much of it is pretty unrealistic. Perhaps the problem is that there are too many karate practitioners who subscribe to the view that there are multiple applications to every move in kata. This sort of view is only a small step—a little sliding step, if you will, because it's a slippery slope—from the notion that a technique can mean anything. And it's not too hard in the confines of the dojo with a compliant junior student to make anything work. Or to change certain aspects of the technique shown in kata and say that you're showing hidden techniques or more advanced levels of this or that move.

The way that kata is often performed has compounded the problem. So many of the kata performances one sees may be appealing to the eye— excessive use of dynamic tension, moves that are held too long, overly large and sweeping arm movements—but they only underscore the lack of any real understanding of *bunkai* on the part of the demonstrators. Even otherwise credible and supposedly knowledgeable practitioners of Okinawan karate succumb to the histrionics of this performance paradigm, and all it really does is make the *bunkai* that much harder to "see." Okinawan karate, if done properly, is not very pretty to look at—certainly not very stylish or flamboyant—but it is effective. And it's effective because the kata were created to preserve lethal methods of self-defense, not generic movements to fit any and all interpretations.

Something about this whole dispute, in fact, reminds me of a scene in *Hamlet*. It's one of his later conversations with Polonius. The Melancholy Dane says, quite apropos of nothing, "Do you see yonder cloud that's almost in shape like a camel?" The old man responds, "By the mass, and 'tis like a camel, indeed." To which Hamlet says, "Methinks it is like a weasel." Agreeably, Polonius responds, "It is backed like a weasel." Hamlet then playfully suggests, "Or like a whale," and Polonius knowingly, and famously, says, "Very like a whale." Of course, Hamlet realizes that the cloud in question cannot have all of these qualities—that Polonius is merely agreeing with the poor boy they all think is mad. They humor him for their own ends.

Isn't that the wonderful thing about clouds, these amorphous, evanescent conglomerations of water droplets: they can be all of these things, because in reality they are none of these things. And we know that. It's a game. We're not hallucinating. We are letting our imaginations play with the world around us. And it's perfectly OK—they're clouds. But when it comes to kata and *bunkai,* this approach is questionable to say the least.

There is an old Zen parable about a very knowledgeable teacher who one day comes to visit a Zen master. Ostensibly, he comes for instruction, but right away the Zen master can see that the teacher has come to show off his own knowledge or to test the master. Whatever the case, the master immediately realizes that the teacher has come with a closed mind—that is, he has come with his own set of fully formed expectations. Nevertheless, the master invites him in for tea. After they are seated, the master begins to pour his guest some tea, but he doesn't stop when the cup is filled. The tea flows over the rim of the cup onto the table. Of course at this point everyone—even those who may never have heard the story— can tell that the master will cleverly inform the guest that metaphorically he is like the teacup; he has come already full. And in the mythic world of enigmatic Zen masters, everyone will realize the truth at that moment and experience instant enlightenment ... or else the disgruntled teacher will stalk angrily away in search of someone who knows what he knows and is willing to acknowledge him for it. Cynical but perhaps more realistic.

The story is appropriate, as every martial arts teacher is certainly familiar with students who begin with their cups already full. Once in a while they arrive at the dojo to "test" the teacher, but more often they come in sincerely, even with humility, yet with expectations. Their expectations are filled with preconceptions about karate or just martial arts in general. Sometimes they are able to revise their expectations, but more often than not they just quit and move on, looking somewhere else for something to match their expectations.

This same scenario, though slightly varied, happens even with experienced martial artists. *Their* expectations, however, produce a kind of tunnel vision so that they see only what they have been conditioned to see. Like the old adage about the carpenter who sees the solution to every problem in terms of a hammer and a nail, the karate practitioner who has spent endless hours pounding a punching post *(makiwara)* tends to interpret all kata in terms of punching, blocking, and kicking. How do we bring an open mind, a beginner's mind, to the analysis of kata? How do we make sure that we are not bringing a cup that is already full to the table?

There are all sorts of problems that tend to influence how we interpret kata; our expectations may only be a part of the problem. But admittedly, any analysis of kata that purports to be anything other than a *possible* interpretation will leave the door open to scathing reviews by a host of self-proclaimed experts, and that may be part of the problem. A study not too long ago, in fact, suggested that "we only trust experts if they agree with us."[16]

Kata is, after all, a solo exercise that is meant to mime the movements of paired fighting in the fashion of a boxer shadow-boxing. But this exercise is not just about blocking and punching. Rather, what we see in kata is the blocking and parrying combined with seizing or grappling or tying-up techniques, followed by attacks with the open hands, the forearms, the elbows, the knees, and, in many cases, taking or throwing the opponent to the ground. Certainly this might seem as strange as seeing Marcel Marceau performing the art of pantomime in street clothes on a busy city street. *What is he doing,* we might ask? Of course, if it's "art," some folks reason, we can interpret it as anything we want. But if that's the case, what are the safeguards? Where are the checks and balances?

Lineage might be one answer: check the lineage. But what if the person passing on the lineage didn't know anything? This is a serious question. After all, if we look at how kata applications are interpreted by different schools of Goju-ryu, for instance, we see a lot of different explanations, and each school can argue convincingly for its own lineage. What do these differences then imply?

FIGURE A.5. From left: the author with Takamine and Higa of the Shodokan lineage

One possibility, of course, is that some of these different interpretations are wrong. Some people were not taught what the kata meant and did the best they could with what they had. Or some teachers never passed on what they knew. If we were to apply Occam's razor here, the question would be: Which explanation requires one to jump through the fewest hoops—that some schools have got it wrong, for any number of reasons, or that kata can mean whatever you want it to?

Yet we seem to have an unquestioning faith in our teachers. Of course, one might ask why the interpretation of kata should be accepted solely on faith. The practicality of a martial application should be demonstrable, on the one hand, and how one interprets kata movement should conform to certain martial principles, on the other. We should be able to ask and to see if a particular application is practical or not, and the principles should be apparent. The larger question is why we seem to throw reason out the window when discussing martial arts.

I once attended a seminar where a high-ranking teacher introduced a technique for trapping the blade of a knife between one's palms by clapping one's hands together to stop the attacker's oncoming knife thrust. The seminar participants dutifully set about practicing this "technique" with plastic or rubber knives for the next fifteen or twenty minutes—yet it makes no sense. I asked myself why the students didn't balk at the logic of this teacher's technique or the reality. I can only surmise that we humans generally are quite willing to give over logic in the face of a perceived superior expertise—the teacher is older, tougher, and the lineage holder, the possessor of secrets only hinted at.

If we accept the notion that the original intention of kata was to preserve martial applications, then we need to honestly examine some of the roadblocks that have, over the years, tended to obstruct our ability to see kata applications correctly.

One of these roadblocks is the rather contradictory notion that many people have embraced as readily as the Orwellian concept of doublethink—that kata is both used to preserve technique and hide it at the same time. How can these both be the intention of kata? Yes, there are things that are not immediately apparent; after all, in kata we are seeing only one side of a conversation, so to speak. But to say, as so many instructors do, that a technique is done one way in kata and yet is meant to be applied against an opponent in a completely different way makes absolutely no sense. Nor does the idea that there are different levels of kata interpretation. A teacher may intentionally withhold teaching certain applications for any number of reasons, but it stretches one's credulity to suggest that the kata themselves were created with the intention of hiding techniques.

Another problem is our general tendency toward myopia. Sometimes we are so entirely focused on an individual technique that we don't see the larger picture. It's like the lion in the cage, so distracted by the chair held in its face that it doesn't see the lion tamer who's holding the chair. We take kata apart and only digest it in pieces, as if it were a series of still pictures, each separate movement complete in itself. Perhaps it comes from the mythic misconception that the martial arts is so lethal that a single blow can disable or even kill an opponent. It's difficult to say whether this is an idea sold to a naive public or whether we harbor such delusions ourselves, a willingness to believe in and attach ourselves to some sort of magical view of the world. But when we interpret each individual move in kata as a distinct move, separate and unrelated to the techniques that come before or after it, we are, in a very real sense, failing to see the forest for the trees.

We tend to see mystery where there is only misunderstanding. In the absence of explanation, "secret" or "hidden" techniques *(kakushi te)* have worked their way into the terminology of kata and the imaginations of students. It is tempting to embrace the mystery of kata as an insoluble conundrum even as we attempt to discover its secrets. After all, we are so often reminded that the journey is more important than the destination. But one should certainly be suspect of anything that purports to offer knowledge wrapped in the cloak of mystery. The Wizard of Oz hides behind a curtain woven of just such whole cloth.

What I have found is that much of the confusion in the way we interpret kata techniques seems to be a natural by-product of the way we teach and train karate, the way it has always been taught and practiced. Once we realize this, we begin to see kata a bit differently. We begin to see that each kata within this system is composed of combinations or sequences of techniques that illustrate self-defense scenarios, and in the process, teach the principles of the art.

Some, of course, will argue that there is no way one can be sure that this is correct. I would be the first to admit that not all systems of traditional Asian martial arts seem to have preserved their forms in this manner—showing application combinations. Some systems seem much more guarded, in a way, showing only techniques, like basics, that must be accompanied by the explanations of a knowledgeable teacher. And, of course, we don't have anyone around who was there at the beginning to ask.

The "proofs," I would suggest, are fourfold: one, the techniques of any given kata are not the same in nature—that is, some techniques are entry techniques, some are controlling techniques, and some are finishing techniques; two, the techniques within the kata are self-referential, meaning they show variations within the larger system; three, when looked at in this way, the techniques are more deadly (more effective), which is, of course, the whole point of a martial art; and four, in application, there is no disengagement from the opponent, reinforcing the Okinawan concept of sticking *(muchimi)* or *ippon kumite*—that is, allowing the opponent only one attack. The kata's techniques are consequently more realistic.

FIGURE A.6. Inside the author's barn dojo

People generally see what they want to see, or rather what they expect to see. If they spend long hours in class doing repetitive generic basics comprising chiefly standard blocking, kicking, and punching, when it comes to analyzing kata, they will generally interpret techniques in the same way. What they are used to doing tends to inform everything else. After stretching and warming up, most karate classes begin with repetitions of basic punching and blocking—and why not, since these are techniques that all levels may engage in together? We practice *hojo undo* (strength training) exercises, *kote kitae* (arm pounding), walk up and down the dojo floor with the *nigiri game* (gripping jars), and face off with two-person drills. But if the goal is to understand the classical kata, then this sort of basic training, as beneficial as it is, is not enough.

Finally, it is important to remember that Goju-ryu is a martial *art* and a movement art. It is difficult, if not impossible, to describe the intricacies of movement. Movement is always dynamic; it is rarely a finished product. This is nowhere more true than kata, where the real meaning of an application often occurs in the space between techniques. In fact, one of the difficulties past studies of the martial arts have had is their reliance on describing end positions, seeing kata and the applications of kata movement as a series of still photographs. Much is lost when this is done.

But in writing about kata or attempting to describe its applications in book form, it is difficult not to succumb to these limitations. In order to describe movement, we must give it a name; we must call it something even if we know that what we say is only part of the truth. So we describe moves as blocks or punches or kicks. But as the teacher will so often explain in the dojo, "a block is not always a block, and a punch is not always a punch." However, even in saying this, one must caution against simply reversing the statement, as is often done, by suggesting that punches are actually blocks and blocks are actually punches. This too is an oversimplification. Goju *bunkai* is far more interesting and diverse. This is not meant to be needlessly cryptic or confusing but to succinctly describe the nature of *bunkai* and kata movement. The only real danger is if we forget that things are not always what they seem.

FIGURE A.7. One of the intermediate techniques from Kururunfa kata

Different schools, however, may use different terms and kata may vary slightly from school to school. Any discussion of kata in text form, therefore, is not necessarily intended as an instructional manual for the uninitiated. My descriptions of kata movement, as brief as they are, are sufficient, I hope, to explain the *bunkai* found within the kata. It is not my intention to act as a proxy for the teacher or to raise a whole new generation of paper dragons, students who spend more time reading about martial arts than practicing it. No book could be or even should be looked at as a substitute for getting out on the dojo floor and actually training. I was raised on this notion and gladly pass it along.

If we do not practice according to the applications of the principles, we can work forever without developing a superior art.[17]

Nor do I wish to suggest that this is yet another series of *bunkai* to add to what already seems a bit burdensome and overwhelming, an almost encyclopedic collection of possible kata applications one can glean from books, magazines, and internet videos. This is not my intention. Rather, I have come to believe that a good deal has actually been lost in the practice of Goju-ryu kata. What I have been engaged in with my own training and teaching has been a conscious attempt to rediscover these lost techniques and principles of movement—to find, for lack of a better term, the original intent of kata.

How one discovers these principles of movement is the goal of training. It comes back, once again, to kata and *bunkai*. Kata is our connection to the past, to the essence of a martial art. If the kata have been preserved faithfully, then through serious and mindful analysis of kata, we should be able to discover meaning.

The way I am suggesting we look at Goju-ryu is, in a sense, fairly simple. It shows Goju-ryu as a system that makes use of certain martial principles, then gives examples to illustrate these principles, and finally shows variations of these same principles and techniques. An understanding of this does not necessarily make the journey any shorter—one must still practice until the sinews and the muscles and the bones begin to understand the technique—but the idea is to get the feet planted firmly on the right road before setting out on the journey. This is just the first step. The journey of a thousand miles, as the ancient sages said, begins here.

Most nights we would walk down the hill from Matayoshi's dojo late, with the smell of mosquito coils still in the air, tired and hungry. We would walk through Heiwa Dori, feeling the soft tar on the roads, still hot from the day, looking for a late-night soup shop or some place to sit and talk before turning in.

Nowadays, I find myself wishing that I had the opportunity to talk to Matayoshi one more time or wishing I had known then the right questions to ask. But Matayoshi died in 1997. I last saw him when he stayed at my house. It was another hot summer, this time in New England. My teacher, Kimo Wall, was taking Matayoshi on a driving tour of the United States, stopping to teach seminars along the way. That summer, Matayoshi had tried to explain to a friend of mine that there were really three kinds of karate. They were sitting at the dinner table. Matayoshi placed three forks on the table between them.

"Three kinds of karate," Matayoshi said, using Japanese this time. "There's what you teach to students," he said, picking up the first fork and setting it down again. "Then there's what you do for demonstrations," he said, picking up the second fork. "And then there's real karate," he said, pointing to the third fork. I think I know now what he meant. But I wish I could ask him a few more questions about real karate and how they did it in the old days.

FIGURE A.8. Left to right: Kimo Wall, the author, Paul Gorter, and Matayoshi, at Higa Seiko's tomb

1

三戦

SANCHIN

FIGURE 1.1. Beginning posture

SANCHIN, OR THREE BATTLES, is one of two Heishu kata in Goju-ryu, the other being Tensho. Miyagi Chojun sensei considered it a fundamental or *kihon* kata, primarily used to "cultivate a strong physical body," focusing on correct breathing and posture.[1] It has often been said that Miyagi sensei would concentrate on Sanchin training for the first three years of a student's practice, only supplementing training with *junbi undo* (warm up) and *hojo undo* exercises.

In Okinawan karate, the three battles of Sanchin are generally thought of as the mind, body, and spirit. However, in an internet article titled "Meeting with a Fuchow Master," Steve Cunningham suggested that a more traditional reading might be "the battles for the control of the three *ch'i* centers in the body."[2] In the same interview, Fuchow Master Chen goes on to emphasize the training of *jing* (vitality or essence), *ch'i* (breath or energy), and *shen* (spirit), and, in point of fact, this emphasis does not seem so very different from the way the Okinawans view Sanchin, however much this may be based on the arcane concepts of the ancient Taoists. And while there may be a kind of metaphysical aspect to one's training of Sanchin—focusing as it does on breath and posture in a way not so dissimilar from yoga or *zazen* in Buddhist meditation—there are also important and fundamental elements of self-defense evident in Sanchin.

This is not to imply, however, as some people have said, that everything is based on Sanchin or that Sanchin exhibits the essence of Goju. There's basic stance (Sanchin *dachi*). There's a straight punch and a closed-fist middle-level block—though it is said that Sanchin was originally done with open hands, and that it was Miyagi who closed the hands—and a grab and pull in with both hands, and a push out and down with both open hands, and a *mawashi uke*. So at least on the surface, it would be difficult to argue that the techniques of Sanchin kata form the basis of Goju-ryu as it is exemplified in the collection of classical subjects that form the canon of Goju-ryu kata. In this vein, some have even gotten into lengthy discussions of *bunkai* for Sanchin. It strikes me as ironic that some folks have taken the kata that, at least by appearances, would seem to be the simplest and burdened it with such undue importance. If I were prone to skepticism, I would say that this sort of implied complexity draped over apparent simplicity merely feeds our natural tendencies to look for the mystical in anything related to the martial arts.

FIGURE 1.2. Opening technique

But there are a few really important things in Sanchin that are often ignored or passed over. One of the most fundamental is the position of the arms throughout most of the kata (fig. 1.1). This position—with the elbow down and the angle between the forearm and the upper arm slightly more than 90 degrees—is fundamental in Goju-ryu, as it is in many martial traditions. Learning to maintain this position, or rather to instantly move into this position—whether the hand is closed as it is in the blocking position of Sanseiru, or open with a vertical hand as it is in Shisochin, or open with the palm up as it is in Kururunfa—is fundamental to good technique and one's self-defense. It's similar to the arm position one sees in Taiji's Ward Off, only in Goju it is done with the elbow down most of the time. The goal should be to maintain the integrity of this structure— with ligaments, tendons, muscles, and bones all involved. Whenever the arm comes up to "block," or rather to intercept, the opponent's attack, this position of the arm is assumed. It is neither too stretched out nor too collapsed—both are weak.

The other aspect to this structure, of course, is the Sanchin stance (Sanchin *dachi*). We usually speak of this in terms of grounding or "down power," as it is sometimes called. In the Chinese martial arts it is often referred to as "rooting," being centered and connected to the ground, with the knees overtop of the feet and the legs held in a kind of structure that a Chinese martial artist might refer to as *peng,* which, of course, is also true of the upper body. It is this structure that is most important in assuming the Sanchin stance. Teachers often focus on gripping the ground by splaying the toes, pushing out with the ball of the foot and pulling in with the heel of the foot, but this is really only a small part of what is going on in this stance. In actuality, the small rotational force expressed through the soles of the feet helps to position the legs correctly in the *peng* structure, solidly rooting the stance and forcing the student to concentrate on dropping one's center and connecting with the ground, as esoteric as that may sound. And it is this structure that the teacher is testing—or more properly, allowing the student to test for him- or herself—when performing Sanchin *shime.*

In one sense, then, this idea of grounding oneself in Sanchin is quite simple; all you have to do is keep your feet under you. I would always say this half-jokingly to my kids whenever we went hiking, especially on steep terrain. It may, of course, be considerably harder to do than it might seem, but I have come to believe that this is a good deal of what Sanchin is about. Balance. Rooting. Sinking. Down power. Lowering your center. How difficult should it be to just stand in Sanchin *dachi* with your hips tucked slightly under and your center of gravity between your feet—from front to back and from side to side—and keep it there as you move and execute fairly simple techniques? Of course, your knees also have to be over your feet and slightly bent, and your spine needs to be straight. It's the same thing that Taiji practitioners are trying to work out when they engage in Pushing Hands, I imagine. It's often said that Kanryo Higashionna was able to stand in Sanchin posture while four people pushed and pulled him from different directions. But in a piece written by Genkai Nakaima, *Memories of My Sensei,* Miyagi Chojun sensei tells the young student that he himself might have "performed Sanchin well only once out of thirty times" he practiced it.[3]

In the martial arts, some of the simplest exercises may in fact be the most difficult to master. Most of us tend to fall forward even when we walk, or we slump and sag and weave wherever we go. Or we work on balance and down power when we do Sanchin, and that's it—that is if we even realize we should be working on balance and rooting and down power and putting our center or mind in the *tanden (dantian)*. Most people's Sanchin is probably too hard, and the focus is on being hard. But martial arts, in many ways, is all about balance.

The second fundamental aspect of Sanchin training is not always practiced, but it has to do with the kata being performed very slowly, though that really has nothing to do with it; it just makes it easier to work on: one should use the whole body in a truly integrated fashion. In other words, each punch and block is moved by the core of the body or by using the *koshi,* if you will. This should not be exaggerated, but neither should the waist or shoulders be locked into place. One should feel this movement when the fist goes out and when it is drawn back. This is practiced in Sanchin, when one first begins training karate, because all movements should employ the body in this fashion. To paraphrase the Chinese classics, the waist is like a millstone, and the arms and legs merely follow.

FIGURE 1.3. Ending open-hand posture, which one can also find in Seisan

So, that being said, what are the three battles beginners must fight in Sanchin kata? Are they mind, body, and spirit, as students have always been told? Isn't everything mind, body, and spirit? Perhaps they are (1) how one breathes, gathering and directing one's energy; (2) how one moves, using the *koshi,* with a supple waist; and (3) how one maintains the integrity or position of the body, especially the position of the arms and legs.

Training in Gibo Seiki sensei's dojo in July was hot. Our karate uniforms were often so soaked with sweat that we would wring them out over the balcony after basics. Then we would line up at the back of the dojo and do Sanchin. Gibo sensei would take us to the far end of the dojo before we heard *"Mawatte,"* and, turning around, we would go the length of the dojo again.

FIGURE 1.4. End *mawashi uke.*

I had often heard stories about the training of Sanchin kata. There were the stories of Higashionna Kanryo sensei, the teacher of Miyagi Chojun, who was said to have practiced Sanchin at least a dozen times a day. When he performed Sanchin, it was said, the floor was hot to the touch. Legend has it that Higashionna sensei could not be moved when he stood in Sanchin *dachi* and gripped the floor, his down power was so strong and rooted.

My own teacher, Kimo Wall sensei, reminded me of these stories whenever I saw him do Sanchin—it was so powerful and focused, each part of the body moving in harmony with every other part. We trained Sanchin with that in mind. We practiced walking in Sanchin *dachi*, carrying thirty- to forty-pound logs, or just standing in Sanchin *dachi*, tossing the same logs back and forth—tossing it up ten times, catching it in the crook of the elbow, and then tossing it to a partner. Or we would do Sanchin kata in the snow in the winter as Kimo sensei would perform *shime,* or hard checking. And at demonstrations, of course, we would do Sanchin as Sensei would break six-foot-long boards over our extended arms, stomachs, thighs, or shoulders.

FIGURE 1.5. Practicing Sanchin stepping with the log

But I think what I remember most about this relatively static exercise—a kata that had no *bunkai* or *kumite* (fighting drill) training associated with it and which was slow enough and quiet enough to listen to one's breathing—is that in this exercise, Kimo sensei once told me, "There's always something moving." I have always found that to be a powerful lesson.

2

転掌

TENSHO

FIGURE 2.1. The double open-hand block, the first technique of the last series in Tensho

TENSHO, ROTATING PALMS OR CHANGING PALMS, is the second of the Heishu kata. It was not one of the original kata of Goju-ryu but was incorporated into the curriculum some time later, developed by Miyagi Chojun supposedly as a softer complement to the harder Sanchin. Tensho is seen as a fundamental kata, focusing on breath and posture in a more internal manner, as some have said, and with softer hand motions. And yet to say that Tensho is a fundamental kata in the Goju-ryu system is perhaps a bit misleading for at least two reasons: one, it was developed much later than the other kata in the system, and two, in many Goju-ryu schools it is reserved for high-level practitioners. One of the questions we might ask, then, if we are to understand this in another way, is: What about the techniques of Tensho is fundamental?

In order to even begin to answer that question, we need to know something about the early development of Goju. Miyagi Chojun sensei began training with Higashionna Kanryo sensei sometime around the turn of the twentieth century, more than a hundred years ago. After fourteen or fifteen years of training, he went to China with his friend, Gokenki, a Chinese tea merchant who lived in Naha at the time and trained together with Miyagi sensei in the now famous Ryukyu Tode Kenkyu-Kai. Many of the great karate teachers of Miyagi's generation—teachers who would go on to found their own schools—got together at the Kenkyu-Kai to train and exchange ideas. In any case, while in China, as legend has it, Miyagi saw some hand movements that he found interesting enough to incorporate into a rather simple training pattern, and he called it Tensho. Or, as some sources suggest, he saw a kata called Rokkishu (Six Hands) and adapted it for Goju practice.

Now, one can imagine that fifteen years of training under Higashionna was probably sufficient to learn whatever system it was that Higashionna sensei taught. One can also imagine that Miyagi sensei did a fair amount of talking and training with Gokenki, by some accounts an influential White Crane teacher. Gokenki, in fact, had also been a friend of Matayoshi Shinko, Matayoshi Shinpo's father and a well-known *kobudo* teacher. When the young Matayoshi Shinko went to China to further his study of the martial arts, it was with a letter of introduction from Gokenki, and Shinko ended up staying with Gokenki's family in Fuchow.

There he studied with both Gokenki's father and with Roshi Kingai, a friend of the family. He brought back with him what would be known as Kingai-ryu or the Golden Bird style, though it is unclear whether Shinko would teach the system to his son Shinpo or send him off to study with his old friend Gokenki.[1]

All of these historical connections raise some interesting questions about the origins of Tensho kata. Did Miyagi sensei see something on his trip to China with Gokenki, as legend has it, or was he already familiar with these techniques—things he may have trained in the Ryukyu Tode Kenkyu-Kai? Was Gokenki, or by extension Kingai-ryu, an important influence on Miyagi?

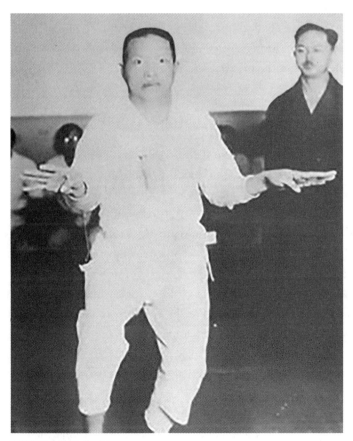

FIGURE 2.2. Gokenki

Matayoshi Shinpo, a generation removed from Gokenki and the early pioneers of karate, learned *kobudo* from his father, Shorin-ryu from Kyan Chotoku, and Goju-ryu from Higa Seiko. He taught some of his senior *kobudo* students kata from the Kingai-ryu system, but he never set out to formally teach any of the empty-hand systems that he knew. He would, however, often demonstrate Kingai-ryu kata, and what becomes immediately apparent is that many of the hand movements bear a striking resemblance to the movements of Tensho kata.

Aside from historical questions, though, the creation of Tensho—the addition of another kata to the Goju-ryu syllabus—raises other questions. What was it about the techniques we find in Tensho that was so important to Miyagi sensei that he felt it necessary to include them in his Goju-ryu curriculum? The assumption is, of course, that there is no need to make a new kata that merely duplicates things that can already be found within a system. So the question is, What did Miyagi sensei feel was missing? What is so unique about the movements of Tensho?

The Techniques of Tensho

The Higa or Shodokan version of Tensho begins from the double-arm *kamae* posture (fig. 2.3), with three, slow Sanchin-like punches and three forward steps in Sanchin *dachi,* though not all schools subscribe to starting the kata this way. Then the kata goes into a series of upper-level, middle-level, and lower-level open-hand blocks and attacks executed first with the right hand, then with the left, and finally with both hands, with two additional steps forward. The kata then finishes with two retreating steps and two palm-up–palm-down blocking techniques reminiscent of Seisan kata, though the number of blocks sometimes varies, concluding with an additional step back with a final *mawashi uke.*

The opening posture of Tensho is certainly significant. The double-arm *kamae* posture is found in Sanchin as well as four of the other classical kata of Goju-ryu. The posture itself reminds us that Goju-ryu is a close-in system of self-defense; it mimics, in solo form, the position one adopts in grappling with an opponent. This is important if we are to understand the techniques of Tensho as anything more than a method of cultivating "a strong physique while encouraging a *budo* spirit," something Miyagi had said in reference to the practice of *kihon* kata. However, it is hard to believe that he would have developed a kata devoid of martial application. Certainly the focus here has always been placed on posture, breath, skeletal alignment, muscular development, and so on—physical and spiritual development rather than the practice of clearly defined self-defense scenarios—but this does not preclude the fact that the movements themselves were obviously martial, with very real applications in mind, even if those applications were not the avowed purpose of the kata or were not stressed at the time.

There were certainly reasons to downplay the martial nature of the classical kata, not just Tensho. The 1936 meeting of karate masters, government officials, and journalists sponsored by the Ryukyu Newspaper Company, and largely organized by Nakasone Genwa, seems to capture this sentiment and highlight the intersection of martial artists attempting to preserve an ancient art amid the political and societal pressures of a changing world. Miyagi sensei himself had, in an earlier essay, emphasized that "training karate-do improves one's health" and that "physical and mental unity develops an indomitable spirit."[2] These, however, are ancillary benefits. The techniques themselves are still martial.

FIGURE 2.3. Double-arm *kamae* posture, which begins Tensho

The template for Tensho seems to have been Sanchin. The double-arm *kamae,* the stepping pattern, the stances, the ending *mawashi uke,* and the palm-up–palm-down blocks suggest that the kata was constructed over the basic framework of Sanchin. Whether this was used merely for convenience or to emphasize the *kihon* nature of the kata, as Miyagi saw it, is not clear. Perhaps it was constructed this way because of its perceived complementary nature. There are obvious similarities to other Goju kata—notably the palm strikes, knife-edge attacks, and open-hand blocks—but there are also differences.

The most obvious difference is that the hand techniques in Tensho— other than the fact that some of them are distinctly White Crane (or Kingai-ryu) in appearance—are executed off the front foot, unlike so many of the attacking hands in the other kata. Tensho also lacks any real movement of the feet in relation to the hand techniques—that is, the hands move independently of any stepping or turning of the body. This is very different from what we generally see in the classical Goju-ryu kata, where blocking and attacking is usually accompanied by very clear stepping or turning patterns that illustrate the principle of off-line move-ment. The third difference is that the blocks and attacks are executed with the same hand, unlike most of the initial entry techniques we see in the classical subjects where the defender generally blocks with one hand and attacks with the other simultaneously.

Taken all together, these differences suggest that the techniques of Tensho are meant to be used as inside counterattacks. That is, the grappling or clinch position may be the best way to explain not only how the techniques should be employed but also the construction—or more properly, the structure—of the kata. Tensho is a composite of fundamental techniques in the sense that these are blocks and strikes, not sequences of receiving, controlling, and finishing techniques but quick hand responses when the defender is unable to move to the outside of the attack. And since the power of the counterat-tack is not generated by one's movement or turning, the short or abbrevi-ated movement that occurs between the block and the attack in the Tensho techniques suggests that Tensho relies on one's ability to understand and use what some have called "short power," or *fa jing* in Chinese terms. This concept of "short power" or *fa jing* would seem to strengthen its claims of being derived from White Crane kung fu or alternatively Kingai-ryu.

In one sense, it seems needlessly pedantic to describe applications or explain *bunkai* for techniques that are not shown in specific application sequences. The techniques of the other classical kata of Goju-ryu, the Kaishu kata, are shown in very specific scenarios, so it is easy to say, for example, that the *mawashi* technique at the end of Saifa kata is used to twist the head; we have the sequence of moves—the entry technique, the bridging technique, and the finishing technique—to bolster or confirm any given interpretation. But Tensho, like many of the techniques in Suparinpei, is a collection of fundamental techniques. To suggest a specific interpretation is merely to give one example, and should be understood in that way.

Keeping that in mind then, the first of these techniques in Tensho is an open-hand block (fig. 2.4) followed by a knife-edge *(shuto)* attack (fig. 2.5). This is the first of four blocks and attacks, if we discount the opening punches, the palm-up–palm-down blocks, and the *mawashi uke,* all of which are reminiscent of either Sanchin or Seisan; in other words, if we just consider the core techniques of Tensho or the techniques that really differentiate it from the other classical subjects, then there are really only four blocks and four attacks.

FIGURE 2.4. First blocking grab

FIGURE 2.5. First attack: *shuto*

Curiously, however, Miyagi sensei did not pair all of the blocking techniques with what would seem to be their attendant attacking techniques. Instead, we find that the first open-hand block is followed by three open-hand strikes—a *shuto* to the neck or head (fig. 2.5), an open palm to the face (fig. 2.7), and a lower-level palm strike to the abdomen or groin (fig. 2.9). Why not put the blocks and attacks together? Why not follow the rising wrist block with the palm strike to the face? Why not follow the downward wrist block with the lower-level palm strike? The middle-level outward wrist block *is* followed by the middle-level palm strike. Why is it that only the first block and attack and the fourth block and attack are paired together in what would seem to be their logical order?

The answer may be in the starting *kamae* posture. From this position, the defender's first response would logically seem to call for some sort of deflection or grab and pulling of the opponent's arm. This pulling motion, used to upset the opponent's balance, would then necessarily be followed by one of the three open-hand attacks—the knife-edge to the neck, the open palm to the face, or the lower-level palm strike to the stomach or groin. It should also be noted that when these techniques—both the pulling block and the attacking palms—are executed off the front foot, with both the defender and the attacker in a right-foot-forward basic stance in the clinch position, then the defender is attacking the opponent's "open door," as it is called in some Chinese martial traditions; that is, the direction of the defender's initial pulling grab and the attacking palm strike are meant to attack the opponent's center at the most vulnerable point, the point at which balance is hardest to maintain.

The next two techniques in the kata are an upper-level or rising wrist block (fig. 2.6) and a lower-level or dropping wrist block (fig. 2.8). Each of these blocking motions would seem to have a corresponding attack—the upper-level palm strike in the first instance and the lower-level palm strike in the latter. Each of these blocking motions would also seem to offer a different way to deal with the opponent's arms from the clinch position, if they are blocks. Because this is a kata composed of fundamental techniques, rather than application sequences or

FIGURE 2.6. Rising wrist block

FIGURE 2.7. Palm strike

FIGURE 2.8. Dropping wrist block

FIGURE 2.9. Lower palm strike

scenarios where the entry, bridging, and finishing techniques are clear, it may be difficult to say with certainty which techniques are only blocks and which are only attacks. Logic would suggest that since the first (figs. 2.4–5) and fourth (figs. 2.10–11) techniques are clearly paired, there is an implied pairing of the other techniques as well. On the other hand, there may be no logical order, and trying to superimpose some sort of logic or specific application on fundamental techniques that may be employed in a variety of ways is very much like trying to pound a square peg into a round hole—something will be lost in the process. In the end, the answers will probably be found, as they usually are, on the dojo floor.

The kata finishes with a series of two, or sometimes three, palm-up–palm-down blocks (figs. 2.12–13)—the same blocks we see executed with a forward slide step and knee kick in Seisan kata—and a final *mawashi uke*. Again, these are techniques shown without the context of an application sequence, but one can imagine them functioning the same way they do in the classical subjects. The double-arm *kamae* posture is the key. The

FIGURE 2.10. Outward wrist block

FIGURE 2.11. Middle-level palm strike

palm-up–palm-down block and the *mawashi uke* in basic stance are both used as releases against the opponent's clinch. In the case of the palm-up–palm-down blocks, the defender keeps the elbows down while bringing both hands up to the outside of the opponent's arms, into the palm-up position, and then, without pause, rotates the hands, palm down, to push against and release the opponent's clinch, or, with the defender placing both arms over the opponent's arms, to assume a position of advantage and follow up with an attack. In Tensho kata, these palm-up–palm-down blocks are executed with a retreating step in basic stance, which may be necessary depending on how firmly the opponent is holding the defender's arms.

And finally, the *mawashi uke* in basic stance—as in Suparinpei, but different from the way it is applied in the classical subjects when we see it used in conjunction with the cat stance *(neko ashi dachi)*—is also a release against the opponent's clinch (fig. 2.14). In this case, the opponent's arms are folded in and the defender's lower hand comes under the opponent's arm, turning the opponent in order to continue with an attack.

FIGURE 2.12. Palms brought up to the outside of the opponent's arms

FIGURE 2.13. Palms covering the opponent's arms

FIGURE 2.14. *Mawashi uke* used against the clinch

As we caught the bus out of Naha, headed to Gibo sensei's dojo for the first time, we were excited and a little nervous. This would be our first experience of training karate in an Okinawan dojo under an Okinawan teacher. Gibo sensei was a friend of Matayoshi sensei's and had been a *kobudo* student of his for many years, as were many of the high-ranking Shodokan teachers.

The dojo was on the second floor of Gibo sensei's house. We could hear the children's class just finishing up as we climbed the stairs. Then there was a mad rush as they slipped on their shoes at the entrance and ran out. We bowed and walked in and stood in the back. The dojo was quite large by Okinawan standards. It must have been thirty feet long and almost as wide. There were mirrors everywhere. At the back of the dojo was a board with the names of the different members written on small rectangular pieces of wood. Nearby was a board with the names of the different kata and the requirements for each rank. I noticed that Tensho was reserved for high-ranking black belts, which surprised me at the time.

In one corner there was a small cloth screen on wheels where people could change. But there weren't any women training that night, so we changed in the back and stowed our bags under the folding chairs that lined the rear wall. I looked around as we began to stretch out before class. There was a cold tea dispenser in the far corner, filled with barley tea. Tucked into the other corner, to the right of the shrine, there was a straight-back chair. By the entrance, over on the side, there were footprints outlined on the floor in Sanchin *dachi*, perhaps for beginners to follow as they learned how to walk in basic stance.

Then came the familiar *"Shugo,"* and we all lined up, knelt, and went through the formal rituals of class. One didn't really need to know Japanese in order to follow along. It all seemed familiar. We went through a series of stretching exercises and then did basics—blocks, punches, and kicks. The senior student called out commands, and each of us counted in turn. We could hear Gibo sensei just outside the back door, hitting the *makiwara*.

When basic exercises were finished, Gibo sensei led us through kata, making corrections and demonstrating various techniques. There were a

FIGURE 2.15. Gibo sensei (left) with the author

lot of things to remember—little things for the most part, but differences that we tried to incorporate as we repeated the kata. Junior students followed along in the back as best they could. We started with Sanchin, up and down the floor until Gibo sensei had us turn around. Then, after all of the other kata, we finished with Tensho.

I remembered from the subject list that Tensho was a high-level kata in Shodokan, so I was a little surprised that we were doing it. There were differences here as well. I've thought about those differences over the years and why Tensho was considered such a high-level subject. Was it merely out of respect for Miyagi Chojun sensei, or was the kata itself somehow more difficult than it seemed?

The Shodokan version of Tensho begins with three Sanchin-like punches, perhaps to allow the practitioner to better understand the differences between the two kata, Sanchin and Tensho. Goju-ryu, of course, takes its name from the line in the "Hakku Kempo" (The Eight Laws), a poem that Miyagi Chojun sensei was said to have been particularly fond of:

Ho wa goju wo tondo su.
"Everything in the universe is breathing hard and soft."

It is, in fact, a good way to make sure one is properly grounded, with good posture, since one should already be familiar with the lessons of Sanchin and should, of course, be bringing this same practice of proper breath, stance, and coordination into each kata. By the time we encounter Tensho kata, these lessons should be largely ingrained, allowing the student to focus on some of the other unique aspects of the kata. It may have found its way into the performance of Tensho simply as a reminder of the hard and soft nature of Goju-ryu. And, of course, it has long been understood, as difficult as it may be to put into one's practice, that the two concepts, hard and soft, are not really separate. In that sense, the execution of the Sanchin-like punches in Tensho may be very different from the punches we see in Sanchin itself.

Thinking back on training Sanchin and Tensho, and all of the other kata that we trained in Gibo Seki sensei's dojo, I'm reminded of a print Matayoshi sensei once gave me. It was a beautiful piece of Japanese calligraphy that he signed and then affixed his stamp to. When I got home,

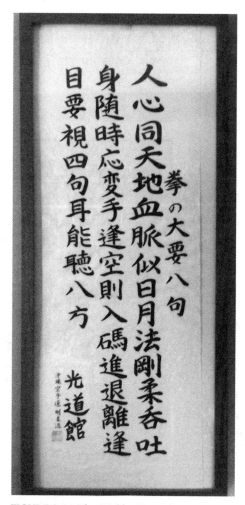

FIGURE 2.16. The "Hakku Kempo"

I had a frame made for it and hung it in the study. I made a copy of it to hang in the dojo. The large kanji on the print is 心 *(kokoro)*, meaning spirit. He had said earlier, over dinner one night, that *kokoro* was the most important thing in training martial arts, so the print with his signature was special to me. But when I got home, back to the States, I noticed that there was a small red stamp in the corner. I asked a number of people that I had in class who could read Japanese what it said, but no one could read it. Someone suggested that it might be Chinese, so I took it over to the university and located a professor of Chinese. He said it was ancient Chinese. It read, "Hard soft not two." He looked at me quizzically and asked, "Does that make sense?" Yes, I thought, it makes perfect sense.

FIGURE 2.17. Kokoro

3

砕破

SAIFA

FIGURE 3.1. Cat stance posture from Saifa

SAIFA KATA IS THE FIRST KATA usually taught in the classical canon of Goju-ryu in most schools, aside from Sanchin, of course. Though there is some evidence to suggest that this was not necessarily the case when Miyagi Chojun sensei was teaching—oral tradition maintains that after some period of time practicing Sanchin kata, a student was taught whichever kata seemed to be appropriate to his needs and physical condition—there seems to be nothing in the kata itself that would with any certainty relegate it to its initial or beginner status. Perhaps the movements are, in some sense, easier to perform. Perhaps the applications or *bunkai* of the Saifa techniques were deemed either less violent or more likely to be encountered in one's first introduction to self-defense. Or perhaps it was simply shorter than the other kata.

In any event, other than the fact that one has to begin somewhere, one shouldn't look at any one kata that is a part of a system as lesser in value or not as important to study. There are techniques in Saifa that do not occur in any other kata in the Goju-ryu system. There are also situations a defender may find him- or herself in—as there are in each of the classical kata of Goju—that are unique to this particular kata.

The name of the kata is generally translated as "to smash and break or destroy"; however, this, or in fact any of the numerous variations on this theme, sheds little light on the actual techniques or applications of the kata movements, as is true of most of the translations of the kanji names of the other Goju-ryu subjects. In fact, most of the name translations serve merely to add to the mystique of karate kata rather than to enlighten the practitioner. The questions they give rise to will, no doubt, remain unanswerable.

I once came across an internet forum post where a couple of students were discussing kata themes and names. One person had begun the discussion, suggesting not only that kata had themes but that they had "personalities" that made them all distinct. The other agreed. This prompted the junior student to ask what the other thought about Saifa. The senior student answered by saying, and I quote, "I'm thinking the name pretty much says it all ... you know, 'to destroy and defeat.' The first three moves," he added, "are the signature of the kata." To this, the junior student responded, "Yeah, that helps when I'm visualizing techniques."

That being said—though I'm not exactly sure if anything of value was said there—what is apparent is that Saifa kata is composed of three, or perhaps four, application sequences and shows certain structural similarities to other kata in the Goju system. For example, it begins with a short sequence of movements that is repeated three times. This repetition of three at the beginning of a kata is also found in Seiunchin, Shisochin, Sanseiru, Seisan, and Suparinpei. Like Seiunchin, however, and unlike the other four kata, this is a *bunkai* sequence—that is, different from the fundamental techniques like the punches at the beginning of Seisan, the techniques at the beginning of Saifa illustrate an application against a very specific attack, a same-side wrist grab, or, as in the first move, the attacker's left hand grabbing the defender's right wrist.

This, of course, raises the obvious question of why Saifa and Seiunchin show the repetition of a specific *bunkai* sequence rather than the repetition of a fundamental technique, like the opening forearm technique, for instance. In other words, why isn't Saifa structured more like Seipai, which opens with a single *bunkai* sequence? Or like Kururunfa, which only shows two opening techniques, one to the right and one to the left (or vice versa)? The easiest and most likely explanation, perhaps, is that the various kata of Goju-ryu came from different sources at different times. They may have always been a part of the same system, especially since they seem to conform to the same principles, but they may have been created by different people, each structured or put together along individually idiosyncratic lines.

This, too, will no doubt remain a puzzle, open to endless speculation, but it is at the very least useful to be aware of how the various kata are structured. It only really matters for one's understanding of the principles of kata analysis. There is no real need for Saifa and Seiunchin to repeat their respective opening sequences. After all, it is easy enough to practice the "other side" of any technique on one's own or outside the performance of kata. In fact, it is probably imperative to do so. But neither is kata sacrosanct, once one understands its structure, and in the case of Saifa, the kata would perhaps be better understood if the beginning was more like Seipai and less like Sanseiru or Seisan with their repetition of threes, repeating basic techniques instead of a *bunkai* sequence.

For some, a discussion of kata structure adds little to their understanding of *bunkai*. As one of my students often suggests, it can seem much like an argument over how many angels can fit on the head of a pin.

But understanding the structure of kata is at the root of understanding *bunkai*—you can't really do one without the other.

So what is essential to understand about Saifa kata?

First Sequence

In the opening sequence, the defender (the one doing kata) is responding to a same-side wrist grab—the attacker's left hand grabs the defender's right wrist (fig. 3.3). Some might suggest that each sequence of Saifa kata begins with a response to a same-side wrist grab. While this is certainly a very real possibility—that this is one of the themes of Saifa kata—this sort of variation in the initial entry technique does not substantially alter the rest of the sequence in most cases. There is little, in fact, to argue definitively how the opponent is attacking in most kata, whether the blocking or receiving technique is against a punch, a grab, or a push. In this case, convention suggests that the attack is a wrist grab.

FIGURE 3.2. First kata position

There are two important points to keep in mind when discussing wrist grabs: One, the attacker is not necessarily *initiating* an attack by grabbing one's wrist; and two, in order to utilize the precarious position the attacker puts himself in by grabbing one's wrist, one should insure that the attacker cannot let go before the defender is in control of the situation. In reference to the first point, it seems unlikely that one would allow an aggressor to grab one's wrist and exert any sort of control before responding to it; however, it is very likely that an aggressor would grab one's wrist or arm at some point in an extended confrontation, particularly in close quarters. In reference to the second point, one certainly wants to escape or release the grab, but without allowing the attacker to let go and continue the attack with another aggressive action. So the first thing we see is that the left hand is brought over simultaneously to trap and begin to release the opponent's hand. The trapping is done by simply placing the left hand on top of the opponent's hand (fig. 3.4). The release is done by squeezing the opponent's hand at the same time. It should be noted that the kata teaches this technique because in the solo kata form, the left hand is wrapped around the right hand (fig. 3.2).

FIGURE 3.3. First technique: Securing the opponent's hand

FIGURE 3.4. Close-up of hand-on-hand position

FIGURE 3.5. Dropping the forearm over the opponent's arm

Once the hand is trapped, the right elbow is brought up, over, and down on the opponent's left arm (fig. 3.5). This is the essential movement of this technique—how we control and bring the opponent's head down—but it is facilitated by stepping forward along a diagonal line to the front and alongside the opponent. Additionally, one should note that there is a wrist lock and twisting of the opponent's wrist applied here.

This is really a fundamental or essential movement to understand because it shows the use of the defender's elbow in escaping from the opponent's control of the defender's hand or lower arm. In other words, anytime the attacker is exerting pressure on the lower arm in this way, left on right or right on left, below the elbow, rather than fighting against the pressure, the defender can yield to the pressure and bring the elbow up and in, over the attacker's arm. Of course, it's important to remember that this is only one of the ways that Goju kata show how to deal with this scenario, and one shouldn't limit one's self-defense to a single kata or a single technique.

STEPPING IN KATA

It may be useful here to digress for a moment to discuss stepping and movement in general, as these are the first steps one takes as a beginner in the study of Goju-ryu.

In one sense, kata is terribly restricting, in the way that we introduce it to beginners—and we were all beginners once. When you add the study of bunkai, it's like putting the cart before the horse. Deriving bunkai from this kind of overly stylized, restrictive movement is an exercise in frustration, at the very least. In the world of art, we say that something is stylized when it is bound by convention and presented in a nonnaturalistic form—much like kata. Of course, I'm referring to the performance of the moves in kata and not the techniques themselves. For example: you want your child to draw, so you give him or her a coloring book instead of a blank piece of paper. What's wrong with that? It provides a little bit of guidance. You can even purchase books that might appeal to different children—a Spiderman coloring book for one and a Little Mermaid coloring book for another. You can already see where this is going, but the not-so-hidden stereotyping is only part of the problem. I think, at least philosophically, we realize that coloring books restrict creativity. Pablo Picasso once said that it took him "four years to paint like Raphael, but a lifetime to paint like a child," and I don't think he meant anything like using coloring books.

So we teach a student that the first step in Saifa kata is to advance along an imagined northeast diagonal line with a right step into a long front stance (zenkutsu dachi). Then the left foot is brought up to the right into a stance that the Japanese call musubi dachi (heels touching with the feet splayed at 90 degrees), as the hands pull back across the chest. Yet this is a sort of stilted, overly stylized movement—completely unnatural—that would never be done in such a punctuated manner if one were actually using the technique against an opponent. And the problem is that this kind of stylized movement, learned at an early stage in our training, generally informs most people's bunkai as well.

Obviously, it is easier to teach the seemingly arcane movements of classical kata when they are broken down—almost like still photographs—and presented in punctuated and highly stylized form, with as little individual variation as possible, especially when one is teaching groups. But once the movements are learned, all of this stiff, robotic, and metronomic movement should be abandoned.

Yet watch any demonstration or performance of kata, and you will see this overly stylized kind of movement. Sometimes I try to imagine what kata performances would look like if we taught bunkai before we taught kata. Let a student practice the technique against a partner for a year before he or she is taught the solo form. I wonder what it would look like? I wonder if the movements would look more natural? I wonder if the artificial gaps and pauses would disappear? Kata performance might allow for more variation and individuality. The only criteria for judging someone's kata would be whether they understood what they were doing and whether they could apply the techniques effectively. It may take a lifetime to learn to move as naturally as a child, but this should really be the goal: to move naturally. Bunkai should follow kata, but kata should be done like bunkai.

It is important to keep in mind that the whole point of entry techniques is to place oneself in a position of relative safety; that is, to move in a way that only allows the attacker the one initial attack. The point of the controlling or bridging techniques—aside from maintaining this position of relative safety—is to get to the head or neck, the most vulnerable and lethal targets. In this first sequence of Saifa kata, this is why it is important to bring the arm up, over, and down on the opponent's arm, not just horizontally across the attacker's elbow as if one is executing an arm-bar. If you simply attack the elbow from the side, it only takes the slightest bend or dropping of the elbow by the opponent to frustrate the attack and protect the elbow. On the other hand, if you bring the elbow up and over the opponent's arm, it doesn't really matter whether the opponent's arm is locked at the elbow or bent; the point is not to fight the arms but to get to the head. Once the head is brought down, the left hand releases its grab, reaching over to grab the opponent's head or hair. Then, stepping back into horse stance *(shiko dachi)*, the right forearm is brought down on the back of the opponent's neck (fig. 3.6).

FIGURE 3.6. Striking to the neck with the forearm in the first sequence of Saifa

It should be noted, of course, that this last point, the forearm strike, raises all sorts of issues, because in most schools this technique will be referred to as *uraken uchi,* a back-fist strike, instead of a forearm strike. The kata looks the same, or very nearly, when it's done, but the *bunkai* is very different. How are we to know which is correct or which is the original intent? To answer this—in fact, to address this question wherever it comes up in the analysis of kata—one should ask which interpretation best conforms to martial principles, which is more realistic, and which is more lethal, because Goju-ryu was never meant to be employed in modern-day point tournaments. In the first case, the principle here is to move in such a way that doesn't allow your opponent a second opportunity to attack. In the second case, it is more realistic because you are using the response of the opponent to your first counter to bring the head down. And finally, it's more lethal because you are attacking the opponent's neck rather than giving him or her a bloody nose with an *uraken* or, as I've seen in some cases, a rap to the chest with a back-fist, which is just plain annoying.

All of this should, of course, be executed without gaps—that is, the entire sequence should be performed in a fluid manner, without pausing between the various techniques, as we frequently do when we teach these same movements or when we perform them in class or for demonstrations. It should also be noted that the force of the forearm strike to the back of the opponent's neck is facilitated by the defender's drop into horse stance and the counter motion or rotation of the waist as the defender moves from the left-hand head grab, with the waist moving in one direction, to the right forearm strike, as the waist snaps back. In other words, the arms should not move independently from the waist or *koshi.*

Second Sequence

Most schools will end the first sequence with the forearm strike to the neck in horse stance. There would seem to be a natural break here, and the dropping forearm attack to the opponent's neck may very well put the opponent on the ground and so end the confrontation. If this is the case, the next sequence would begin with the step forward into cat stance along the northwest angle, while executing a semicircular rising block with the left hand, palm up, and a semicircular descending block with the right hand, palm down. This is an effective block against a two-handed push or, as a release, against a clinch or grapple with an attacker.

If one is stepping to the side of a push, this is a good position from which to kick the side of the attacker's knee (fig. 3.7). The kick functions in such a way as to turn the opponent. From here, one need only grasp the opponent's shoulders, digging the half-fist into the trapezius muscles, and pull the attacker down and back, onto the knee of the front stance. In this scenario, the two blocking and kicking combinations are separated, and the finishing techniques—the pull down and hammer-fist strike—are only shown on the second side. This sort of structure, we will see, is typical of Goju-ryu kata.

However, there may be an equally strong argument to see this sequence—the double "blocking," kick, pull down, and hammer fist—as a continuation of the opening sequence.

While it certainly works fairly well as a double-arm block of an opponent's two-handed push or clinch, there are a number of arguments one could put forward against this interpretation. The first is that the opening structure of both Saifa and Seiunchin seems to be similar, and if this is the case, then one would expect to see more of a finishing technique attached to the third repetition of the opening movements. This is certainly the case in Seiunchin. Another argument is that the kata shows one stepping forward along a northwest or northeast angle. It is the forward angle step, moving as it does into the opponent's attack, if slightly off line, that might suggest another interpretation. It is perhaps just as likely that one could use the two-handed "blocking" motion to twist the head of the opponent after hitting the neck with the forearm attack of the previous move. In this scenario, the two-handed "block," or the use of the rising left palm and the pushing down of the right palm, would begin to twist the head and turn the opponent around, while the kick directed at the opponent's knee—or the knee itself used to attack—would continue to turn the opponent. The next moves of this sequence would be the same—that is, pulling the opponent down onto the defender's front knee and finishing with a hammer-fist attack. The only difference is how the double-arm blocking motion is used.

FIGURE 3.7. Kicking to the opponent's knee to turn him around

It's important to note, here, the use of the cat stance. In this sequence of moves, we generally teach students to step out along a northwest angle into a right-foot-forward cat stance, with both arms describing a sort of half-circle motion, ending with the left palm up and the right palm facing down, although in some schools this step is more of a sideways step.

This position is often held, especially when teaching large groups in the dojo and counting out each movement so that everyone moves together. But again, the unnaturalness and overstylization should be apparent here. If you were actually employing this technique, you would not pause in cat stance. You would move from the previous position, whatever it happened to be (in this case, horse stance) and simply kick. In other words, we have overstylized the weight transition and turned it into a cat stance. The whole point is to shift the weight onto the left leg so that you can kick with the right. How fast would you do this in reality? Do it fast enough, and the cat stance disappears. Do it slow enough, and it becomes another source of endless debate about its purpose and function.

Third Sequence

It is difficult to say whether this is really the second or third sequence of the kata. However, the points one should remember here are that it shows a 180-degree turn, it is against an upper-level attack, and it shows a variation of the previous sequence, without the kicks. Whereas the previous sequence shows kicks being used, at least in part, to turn the opponent around, this sequence shows one stepping to the outside of the attack in order to turn the opponent. The 180-degree turn we see in kata implies that the attack is coming from the west (if the kata begins facing north). By stepping and turning 180 degrees to execute the next technique, the defender places him- or herself in a 90-degree relationship to the attacker. If we were practicing this technique in *ippon kumite* drills—that is, facing each other—this technique would show the attacker stepping in with a left hand, upper level punch, and the defender stepping out with the right foot, while turning 90 degrees to face the attacker from the side as the attack is blocked first with the right hand and then the left coming up underneath (fig. 3.8). The left forearm protects against the attacker's elbow, controlling the attacking arm. The defender's left hand will come to rest on the attacker's left shoulder, while the defender's right hand will come to rest on the rear of the attacker's right shoulder. The attacker is then pulled down onto the forward knee of the front stance—this is often how the front stance is used in Goju-ryu—and finished with the hammer-fist strike.

The most important aspect of this technique, however, and the one that is most often misunderstood, is the function of what has been called a half-fist or clamshell fist (fig. 3.9). This technique is most often interpreted as a strike to the ribs, partly because it is thought that the smaller striking surface of the extended knuckles fits between the opponent's ribs and partly because it looks as though it is executed at the level of the lower chest when it is done in kata. In a sense, this illustrates one of the pitfalls in the interpretation of kata. By disconnecting this technique from what precedes it and from what follows it, the only explanation would seem to be a middle-level strike. The technique that precedes it shows the open hands at shoulder level, pulling down. What looks like a half-fist is actually the hands gripping or digging into the trapezius muscles at the top of the attacker's shoulders (fig. 3.10). It looks as if the half-fist is being thrust out in an attack because of the recoil from a forceful pull down. The finishing technique is the hammer-fist strike (fig. 3.11).

FIGURE 3.8. Turning to intercept an upper-level punch with the opponent stepping in from the west

FIGURE 3.9. The half-fist from Saifa

FIGURE 3.10. The half-fist is used to pull the opponent down.

FIGURE 3.11. The half-fist pull-down is used to drop the opponent onto the forward knee of the front stance.

Fourth or Final Sequence

This final sequence begins with a blocking or receiving technique, a sweep of the opponent's leg, a downward hammer-fist strike (fig. 3.12), and an uppercut. These techniques are shown on both the right and left sides, in response to a right-hand grab or punch and then a left-hand grab or punch, though in all likelihood, since Goju-ryu is indeed a close-in fighting system, the initial techniques here may work best from a clinch or more grappling-like starting position. The finishing techniques, again typical of Goju-ryu kata, are shown only on one side, attached to the second sequence. And direction is also important: the attack is from the west compass point.

In one sense, this sort of structure helps to separate the sequences, to show where they begin and end, because clearly the uppercut is not a finishing technique. However, at times this structure can be misleading. For instance, in this case the next technique is a forward step and block—an advancing step in basic stance with what appears to be a right open-hand mid-level block (fig. 3.14). This in turn is followed by a middle-level punch *(chudan tsuki)*. There are two points to remember here, however: one, the right hand is going from a closed fist to an open hand, which often signifies a grabbing technique (grabbing techniques are indicated when the hand either opens or closes); and two, the kata shows one advancing or stepping forward with what looks like a block, which means that one is already controlling the opponent.

Interestingly enough, these techniques—the hammer-fist strike, the uppercut, the middle-level open-hand block, and the straight punch—may have a far more violent application than what one ordinarily sees being practiced, even in the traditional dojo, simply because appearances are deceiving. In this case, after the sweep and hammer-fist strike on the left side—the defender's right arm being brought down on the opponent's left arm attack while the defender's left forearm attacks to the neck—the fist opens to grab the hair, or the opponent's topknot in ancient times, pulling in as the defender pivots to attack with the uppercut. The defender then steps in toward the attacker, switching hands, and grabs the head with the right hand in order to punch with the left. This is the more obvious and conventional interpretation.

FIGURE 3.12. The sweep and hammer fist begins the last sequence of Saifa kata.

FIGURE 3.13. The first sweep and hammer fist is an incomplete sequence.

FIGURE 3.14. The step into an open-hand middle-level "block"

FIGURE 3.15. Grabbing the chin before the head-twisting straight punch

However, since the defender is already grasping the opponent's hair with the left hand, it is a far more deadly attack—and more in keeping with the techniques of the other classical subjects—if the defender, withdrawing the uppercut and stepping forward with the open-hand "block," brings the attacker's chin around with the step into the right-foot-forward front stance (fig. 3.15). This motion twists the attacker's head in one direction and the left straight "punch" forcefully snaps the head back. Alternatively, the forearm of the uppercut "punch" might be used to attack the opponent's neck, in which case the right open-hand "block" would reach overtop to grab the opponent's chin, with the left straight punch again twisting the attacker's head. These are variations, it will be noted, but the intention of the *bunkai* is the same in either case.

The essential technique here—and the one that is so often misunderstood—is the final technique, often referred to as the *mawashi uke* or *tora guchi* (fig. 3.16). When most people perform this move in kata, it looks as though they are pulling back a vine, plucking a grape, and offering it to a friend, all while standing on one leg. How aesthetically charming and utterly impractical. As interesting as this technique is in appearance—the application potentials seem almost endless sometimes—in the classical subjects of Goju-ryu, it always occurs at the end of a sequence; that is, it functions as a finishing technique. And since we can see that the purpose of the receiving and controlling techniques is to make it possible to get to the attacker's head or neck, the *mawashi uke* in cat stance (really a misnomer, since it is not really a receiving or *uke* technique except in Suparinpei kata) is used to twist the head or break the neck of the opponent (fig. 3.17), as gruesome as that is and certainly impractical to practice with a partner in the dojo.

But the *mawashi uke* technique has been at the center of a lively debate about *bunkai* and kata technique for quite a while now. Sadly, kata structure doesn't seem to enter into any of the arguments, but there is still a good deal of lively debate. One discussion forum post I came across noted that " at the very end of ... Saifa, ... when retreating backward into *neko ashi dachi* and the block *shuto enkei uke* is performed, I have noticed ... that many teachers drop their weight and height as the *shuto uke* is performed." Someone else responded to the implied question, suggesting that "*tora guchi* or *mawashi uke* is a general multipurpose block.... It is usually finished with a two hand press, which can represent a whole plethora of strikes."

FIGURE 3.16. The final mawashi posture of Saifa

FIGURE 3.17. The mawashi technique is used to twist the head of the attacker.

So here is a whole debate of over forty posts on this forum alone over a question of technique and what it could mean in application; that is, a question of *bunkai*. The person that initially poses the question is trying to figure out why some teachers seem to sink into a low cat stance when they do this technique in kata, which is really a question of *bunkai*, or, in other words, what function the low cat stance has in application. The funny thing to me is that sometimes we make all sorts of hidden assumptions that may color the way we interpret kata. This person has already assumed that the technique he is doing is a *shuto enkei uke*. What if it's not? What if it's not a *tora guchi* or *mawashi uke* either? What if it's not a "multipurpose block"? What if it doesn't end with "a two-hand press"? What if it's not a strike at all, let alone "a whole plethora of strikes"? Why would one execute a *shuto* strike in cat stance anyway? It lacks the grounding to have very much power. Someone else goes on to suggest that the cat stance is there for mobility. I have certainly heard that argument before, but is it really as mobile a stance as basic stance? Isn't there any other function of a cat stance that might be more practical—like you use the knee for a knee kick by simply raising it up, or the foot to kick with, since it doesn't necessitate any shifting of weight?

If we suppose, for the sake of argument, that cat stance is really just an indication in kata of a kick, whether it's with the knee or the foot, perhaps that will lead us off into another direction, perhaps even in the right direction. For example, if the knee is attacking in cat stance, then what is it attacking? The most lethal target would be the opponent's head. This begs the question, how do we get the opponent's head into a position where we can attack it with the front knee of *neko-ashi-dachi*? And there we find "*mawashi uke.*" Sometimes the words we use to describe things end up getting in the way.

So, in sum, Saifa kata is a study in a same-side grab release, the use of the cat stance to kick, the stepping and movement we see in the third sequence to move to the outside of an opponent's attack, and the use of the *mawashi* technique.

We were usually woken up sometime around three or four in the morning when the delivery trucks would pull up alongside the market, dropping off vegetables and produce for the market located on the ground floor of an apartment building that Matayoshi Shinpo sensei owned in downtown Naha. It was hard to get back to sleep at that point, with the trucks backing up, the engines left idling, and all of it setting the dogs to barking. Most mornings we would be up and out early, stop to visit with *okusan*, Mrs. Matayoshi, and set off in search of an American-style breakfast. Generally, we would walk up to Matayoshi sensei's house and train after breakfast, if there wasn't something else scheduled, and afterward head over to Ni-kai, an inexpensive lunch counter on the second floor off Heiwa Dori that reminded me of an old Woolworths.

I suppose we were fairly predictable in our routines, but still it often surprised us when Matayoshi sensei would just show up and have tea with us, or drag us off to see the old *sai* maker, or commandeer a van to see the northern side of the island. He always seemed to know where we were. We might be walking along the crowded streets in the middle of a hot afternoon, look around, and there was Matayoshi sensei sitting on the sidewalk curb, smiling but looking as if we had just caught him in a game of hide-and-seek. He might ask us where we were going or just invite us to dinner. He was so unpretentious that it was hard in these casual encounters to remember that this man was recognized by the Japanese government as a Living Treasure.

One afternoon, he took us off to visit a well-known *buyo* (traditional Okinawan dance) teacher. He had been teaching some of her students *kobudo* techniques that they would then incorporate into their traditional folk dances. I had often heard speculations about the close kinship between Okinawa's folk dance and Okinawan karate. There were stories that some of the folk dances had hidden karate moves, disguised by the rhythm and flowing movements of the dance. It was interesting to watch the dancers with this in mind, as Matayoshi sensei took them through a number of sequences from the *eaku* (boat oar) kata. After the rehearsal, my teacher, Kimo Wall sensei, asked me to demonstrate the *eaku* kata, with the miniature *eaku* that the dancers used, for Matayoshi sensei and the *buyo* teacher. It was a less than memorable performance after watching the dancers, I'm sure.

FIGURE 3.18. Matayoshi playing the drum

But a few nights later, Matayoshi sensei took us to an evening *buyo* performance that I remember quite well—a performance with both formal court dances and folk dances, accompanied by a number of musicians and singers. In one dance, a woman came out on stage in peasant dress, carrying a hoe *(kuwa)* over her shoulder. She was accompanied by a single *sanshin,* an Okinawan *shamisen.* I watched her move about the stage as though she was acting out a story about planting and hoeing and harvesting potatoes. Then she stopped in the middle of the stage, turning her back to the audience, and knelt. When she stood up, she had taken her dress off her shoulders and hitched up her skirt, tucking it into the wide cloth belt she wore around her waist. Underneath, she wore a karate *gi* (uniform). She stood in ready posture, feet wide, her left fist clenched, and her whole attitude had changed—her expression fierce. When the music began once more, she was doing *kobudo*—the techniques were strong and clean, with real power, and her *kiai* (spirit yell) was loud, punctuating the music.

FIGURE 3.19. The author practicing *eaku* at the Kodokan
Hombu dojo

I think I must have realized that night that things were not always
what they seemed—clearly something had been hidden here. And if powerful martial techniques could be hidden in a traditional Okinawan folk
dance, what was hidden in kata?

4

制引戦

SEIUNCHIN

FIGURE 4.1. The first position of Seiunchin

SEIUNCHIN IS USUALLY THE SECOND KATA taught in the classical canon of Goju-ryu in most schools, though the order in which any of the classical kata are taught varies considerably from school to school. Even the kanji used for Seiunchin gives rise to a variety of translations, few of which seem to add much to one's understanding of the kata. Some suggest that the correct translation should read "marching far quietly," or "attack far suppress," while others have suggested the wonderfully figurative "blue hawk fight." I would love to imagine that this kata has something to do with blue hawks fighting, but I've never seen a blue hawk and I can't imagine what the moves—many of them very grounded stances in horse stance, far from taking flight—have to do with any bird-like movements, let alone blue hawks. The translation that I think is most helpful and appropriate is "set of pushing and pulling," a translation offered by Higa Seikichi sensei's daughter one night after training in the Hombu dojo, the list of kata posted in kanji on the front wall.

Again, like Saifa kata, Seiunchin should not be considered a beginner's kata, though it is generally taught at green belt or fifth *kyu* level. There are techniques in Seiunchin that do not occur elsewhere in the canon of classical Goju-ryu kata—that is, both the attacking scenarios and the defensive responses *(bunkai)* are, of course, unique, as they are in each of the classical kata.

Some schools, most notably Meibukan, place Seiunchin much later in their syllabi, but thematically, because the majority of its techniques are responses to cross-hand wrist grabs, it seems more appropriate to follow the practice of Saifa, with its same-side wrist grabs, with Seiunchin. In fact, some would argue that each sequence in Seiunchin is an exploration of this theme of cross-hand wrist grabs. And while there are no overt neck-twisting techniques in this kata, like the *mawashi* technique at the end of Saifa, there are violent neck and head attacks in Seiunchin as well.

It may be useful here to emphasize that Goju-ryu is a *system* of self-defense. To some, this will seem as though I'm stating the obvious. However, I don't mean a system in the narrow sense of the word. Practitioners know the story of Jin'an Shinzato, who in 1930 was asked, at a demonstration in honor of Crown Prince Hirohito's succession to the throne, what he called his style. At the time, however, there were no style names as we know them today—people just practiced *"te."* Upon returning to

Okinawa, Shinzato related the encounter to Miyagi, and Miyagi sensei, referencing a line from the "Hakku Kempo" in the *Bubishi,* often called the bible of Okinawan karate, decided to call his *"te,"* Goju or Hard-Soft style. Subsequently, this name was registered with the Dai Nippon Butokai (All Japan Martial Arts Association)—this at a time when karate styles and their respective curricula on Okinawa were not well defined. Naihanchi is just one example of a kata that was practiced early on in both Shorin-ryu and Goju-ryu dojo.

A shared lineage and curriculum is, of course, what defines a system in the narrow sense of the word. But Goju-ryu is a system in a larger sense because the smaller parts, the different kata, all fit together as a cohesive whole that seems neither incomplete nor needlessly repetitive; take any one part or kata out and you will have lost significant pieces of a self-defense repertoire. The canon of Goju-ryu classical kata, from Saifa to Suparinpei, are self-referential, share similar themes, and illustrate the same martial principles. One must study the whole system, I would argue.

Yet stories persist about the early days of training under Miyagi Chojun sensei and how few students were taught all of the classical kata. Rather, it is said, students were first taught Sanchin to develop a "Goju body," and then taught whatever kata seemed appropriate to their body type—Seiunchin being more suitable for a physically small and less muscular karate *ka,* it has been said. This sort of thinking, part of karate lore passed on through oral tradition, seems to suggest that one could rely on a single kata or at best a few kata for one's self-defense. But this misses the thematic nature of kata and really undermines the whole concept of Goju-ryu as a system in the larger sense of the word.

If classical Goju-ryu subjects could be strung together in one lengthy kata, much as in Taiji, perhaps we would avoid this fanciful notion that each kata is somehow self-contained and independent (rather than interdependent), a complete catalogue of self-defense, each open to an almost infinite variety of interpretations and applications. What we do have is eight *bunkai* kata, for lack of a better descriptor, with each kata focused on certain themes and illustrating those themes with examples of self-defense scenarios. Seiunchin demonstrates self-defense techniques against grabs and pushes.

So what is essential to understand about Seiunchin kata?

First Sequence

In the opening sequence, the defender (the one doing kata) is responding to a cross-hand wrist grab—the attacker's left hand grabs the defender's left wrist. Again, just as in Saifa kata, the first technique is both to release the attacker's wrist grab and control the situation so that the attacker cannot initiate another attack. This is accomplished in two ways, both illustrated quite clearly if one follows the movements of the kata. The attacker's grip on the defender's wrist is weakened when the defender moves forward toward the attacker, along the northeast angle. At the same time, both hands are brought up, back-to-back (fig. 4.2).

The important point here is to drop the left elbow as the hands rotate up. As it says in the Chinese classics, "All the joints of the arms should be completely relaxed, with shoulders sunk and elbows folded down."[1] No matter how strong the grip is, the release technique—and this is true for the second sequence of the kata also—is easier to do if one is able to drop the elbow. Dropping into horse stance not only makes this easier to accomplish but also makes it easier to control the opponent as the left hand rotates to grab the opponent's wrist and the right forearm is brought down on the opponent's elbow (fig. 4.3). Dropping into horse stance here helps to bring more force to bear on the opponent's arm, which in turn brings the head down.

FIGURE 4.2. Both hands are brought up back-to-back, releasing the opponent's grip.

FIGURE 4.3. In the second position, an arm bar is used to bring the opponent's head down.

THE PROBLEMS IN TEACHING KATA

It's important to note here that the only difference one should see between the execution of a technique in bunkai and the execution of the same technique in kata is the rhythm or speed of the techniques that make up the sequence—and even this difference is, in fact, arbitrary. When we teach kata, we necessarily slow the movements down, even to the point of separating the feet from the hands. We teach a student to step forward along the northeast angle into a right-foot-forward horse stance. Once the teacher has determined that each student has managed to step forward correctly, the teacher gives the command for the students to execute the next technique—the hands are brought up back-to-back. After the teacher checks to see that each student has indeed brought both hands up—often pausing to make minor corrections here and there—and the angle of the arm is correct, the teacher gives the command for everyone to perform the next move. The problem is that this sort of slow and deliberate movement often becomes ingrained; the students will continue to perform the kata at the same slow pace and with the same punctuated rhythm that was employed when they first learned the kata, and, in the process, often separating the movement of the hands and feet.

A student once wrote to me, asking about the opening move of Seiunchin. She was a good student and a quick learner, but she had been taught the kata in the typically punctuated and deliberate fashion I have described above. Her performance of the kata was creditable, as she tried to perform the kata exactly as she had been taught. What puzzled her was the opening position, a right-foot-forward horse stance with the arms down and the hands out over the knees. She couldn't figure out the bunkai, how this movement was supposed to be applied against an attacker, particularly when the next technique involved bringing the hands up and out, back-to-back. She found the explanation her teacher offered of the first technique, a release against a bear hug from the rear, less than satisfying. She was told that the next technique— bringing the hands up back-to-back—was a release from a two-handed choke, but stepping forward into a choke hold didn't seem to make much sense either. Many schools look at this move as a release against a front two-handed choke simply because both of the defender's hands seem to be doing the same thing. But this is not the case. There are many places in the Goju-ryu classical subjects where appearances are deceiving, where both hands, though apparently doing something similar, are not doing the same thing.

What this illustrates for me is the problems we face in teaching kata. When we first learn kata, the techniques and movements are necessarily disconnected. It's easier to learn if we only have to concentrate on learning one thing at a time. The stepping for this student had been disconnected from the hand movements. It's OK to learn kata this way, but one must keep in mind the purpose of the movements; that is, at some point we need to reconnect the kata with the bunkai. The moment one begins to step forward and drop into horse stance here, the hands begin to move up into the back-to-back position. The attacker doesn't wait for one to drop into horse stance and then bring the hands up. Everything in a sequence must be connected and executed without pause. Any hesitation or gap in a sequence allows the attacker a way in.

The next moves in this sequence should also remind one to keep the elbows down. The left hand continues to hold the attacker's wrist as the hand is brought up to a chambered position. At the same time, the right forearm maintains contact with the attacker's arm as the right open hand is brought up and then rotated to grab the attacker's hair or head (fig. 4.4). At this point, the left hand can release its grip and, with the hand open, attack the neck or throat of the opponent (fig. 4.5). In the next series of moves, the defender's right hand pulls and twists the hair as the left hand controls the opponent's chin, shifting to the left into a kind of right-foot-forward cat stance but with the heel down and the toes up (fig. 4.6). The right foot being drawn in is used to hook the opponent's leg and facilitate turning him or her.

From here, the defender, holding the attacker's chin in the left hand and the hair in the right hand, shifts forward into a right-foot-forward basic stance (fig. 4.7), further twisting the opponent's head, and imme-diately steps back into a left-foot-forward basic stance, driving the right elbow up into the spine of the opponent or twisting the neck (fig. 4.8).

FIGURE 4.4. The right hand is brought up to grab the head while maintaining pressure on the opponent's elbow.

FIGURE 4.5. The left open hand comes in to attack the neck.

FIGURE 4.6. Shifting to the left side, the opponent's head is twisted by pushing up with the left and pulling down with the right.

FIGURE 4.7. Completing the turn around by pushing forward

FIGURE 4.8. Stepping back to attack with the elbow

One of the essential lessons, then, even from this first sequence of Seiunchin kata, is that it is important to follow the kata exactly in order to understand the meanings of the techniques in kata. Yet even when one follows kata movement, appearances can be deceptive, especially when we fail to see the moves in combination or in sequences. The techniques of this sequence are often disconnected, giving rise to elbow attacks to an opponent's chest, assisted punches where the left hand pushes on the right fist, and back-fist strikes against an opponent's wrist grab. The other lesson here, it seems to me, is that the purpose, and indeed one of the principles, of the techniques we find in Goju-ryu is to get to the opponent's head as quickly as possible, and then end the confrontation. We will see this over and over in the sequences of the classical subjects.

Second Sequence

The second sequence again shows a response to an opponent's cross-hand wrist grab. In the first of these, the attacker has grabbed the defender's right wrist with his right hand. There are some schools that imagine kata as one long confrontation with a single opponent, sort of like a Saturday morning grade-B kung fu movie, each attack and counterattack parried and dealt with until the final devastating blow. However, while this is certainly flashy and entertaining and may be a useful, or at least interesting, training method, it seems to contradict some of the fundamental martial principles that the system is based on, not least of which is the idea that how one blocks or receives (the *uke*) the initial attack should place the defender in a position where the opponent cannot attack again. It also doesn't seem to show the controlling and finishing techniques in a sequence—in other words, *bunkai* drills done that way do not demonstrate an understanding of the structure of kata. Without at least some understanding of kata structure, one's understanding of *bunkai* will be superficial at best.

It is often said that the opening technique of this second sequence (fig. 4.9) uses two hands because the defender is particularly strong. While this may be the case, one should not take this to mean that the left open palm is an assisting arm, pushing against the right arm because of the attacker's superior strength. Rather, the left hand is used to "trap" the attacker's hand so that he can't let go. Similar to what we see in the opening move of Saifa kata, the idea here is to release the opponent's grab and make sure we are controlling the situation at the same time (fig. 4.10). Again, this is done in a few ways, but they all have to do with following the kata. Stepping forward into a right-foot-forward basic stance to the northeast, while dropping the elbow and bringing the right arm up, makes it very difficult for the opponent to maintain the grip. At the same time, however, the defender places his or her left hand over the gripping fingers of the attacker (fig. 4.11), pushing out toward his center (fig. 4.12). These techniques, all executed simultaneously, work against the attacker's wrist. The wrist lock will force the attacker to drop to his left—the only option he has to try to release the pressure on the wrist caused by the trapping of the hand.

FIGURE 4.9. The first technique of the second sequence is used to trap the opponent's hand.

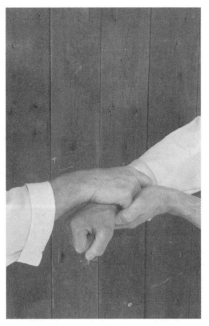

FIGURES 4.10–12. Trapping the hand; close-ups of the trapping hands

Once the defender has the attacker in this position, the defender steps in along the northeast angle, attacking the opponent's head with the left hand and either grabbing the head or hair. The front leg of the horse stance can be used here to further attack the opponent's stance, or the opponent's head can be brought down onto the front knee. Then, stepping back while still maintaining a grip on the opponent's head, retreating into the right-foot-forward horse stance, the right forearm is brought down on the back of the attacker's neck (fig. 4.13).

It should be apparent from this sequence that Goju-ryu, a close-quarters system of self-defense with many grappling types of techniques, will often attack the opponent while stepping back because of the controlling techniques we find in many of the sequences. Some authorities have suggested that, as a rule, advancing kata moves indicate offensive techniques, while retreating kata moves indicate defensive techniques. Clearly that is not always the case, nor should it be seen as a rule to follow in one's analysis of the classical subjects.

FIGURE 4.13. The first "down block" is used to control the opponent, while the second is used to attack the neck.

The other essential point one should remember from this sequence is that the down block, *gedan uke,* sometimes referred to as a *gedan barai,* is not a block at all but an attack. Throughout the Goju-ryu classical subjects, the defender has brought the opponent's head down to attack it with a dropping forearm attack. Regardless of whether we refer to it as a *gedan uke* technique or not, out of habit or merely to employ a familiar term, it is never used as a down block in the classical subjects.

We also occasionally encounter authors who seem to regard kata as an end in itself—that is, as a means to develop and strengthen the leg muscles if a kata employs a number of horse stances, for example, or any number of other ancillary purposes. But there are other exercises that might better be used for these same ends. The movements and techniques of kata should never be divorced from their *bunkai.* The predominance of horse stance in Seiunchin is neither to strengthen the legs nor to provide one with a stable stance most suitably employed against any sort of lateral resistance, as has been said. However effective that might be—and I am reminded of the demonstrations of *shime* testing on students performing the Shorin-ryu kata Naihanchi, another kata that relies heavily on horse stance—the purpose of horse stance is the same in Seiunchin as it is in any of the other classical subjects: it is used to bring opponents down or to attack opponents as they are thrown to the ground. In fact, to use horse stance as an effective means of resistance training or meeting an opponent's force with this sort of imagined immobility or grounding really contradicts the kind of movement we see employed in the classical subjects, where the rule is, more often than not, to get out of the way. If we were speaking of the classical Chinese martial arts, it would be seen as a kind of "double weighting" to meet force with force or to use hard against hard, not at all Goju-like, nor how one should understand the concept of "hard-soft."

Third Sequence

The third sequence shows a response to an opponent's push. The initial receiving technique (fig. 4.14) could certainly be employed against a punch or a grab but seems better suited to an opponent's push, whether the push is from a short distance or a clinch. In either case, however, one of the important points to remember here is that the defender does not have to deal with both arms of an attacker who is pushing with two hands. The defender only needs to block and move to the outside of either arm.

The initial response, as in many of the Goju-ryu sequences, is shown twice, the first one moving to the outside of the attacker's left arm and the second time moving to the outside of the attacker's right arm. In the first instance, the defender blocks with the right and then grabs and pulls the opponent's arm with his left hand, while simultaneously dropping back into a right-foot-forward horse stance as the right hand counterattacks with a *shuto* strike to the ribs. In the second instance, the defender blocks with his or her left and then grabs and pulls the opponent's arm with the right, while dropping into a left-foot-forward horse stance as the left hand counterattacks with a *shuto* strike (fig. 4.15). The finishing technique—a forearm strike and downward elbow attack—is shown only after the second receiving technique (fig. 4.16).

FIGURE 4.14. First position of the third sequence

FIGURE 4.15. Dropping down to attack the opponent's ribs

FIGURE 4.16. Downward elbow attack

Another somewhat unique characteristic we find in the first two kata of the classical subjects Saifa and Seiunchin is the predominance of forearm striking techniques, rather than the much more characteristic head-twisting techniques we see in the other kata. The exception, of course, is the *mawashi* technique at the end of Saifa. In Seiunchin, however, we see the repeated use of forearm strikes as finishing techniques, reinforcing the importance of *kote kitae* (sometimes called arm-pounding) training with a partner in doing preparatory or conditioning exercises.

Fourth Sequence

The fourth sequence seems to work equally well against a two-handed push or a cross-grab, but is perhaps best seen in a clinch or grappling attack where both the attacker and the defender are using both hands (fig. 4.18).

FIGURE 4.17. The initial technique of the fourth sequence

FIGURE 4.18. Many of the techniques begin from this initial position.

It's important to remember, and certainly worth repeating here, that Goju-ryu is a close-in fighting style. Many of the techniques appear to begin from a clinch or grappling position, with both hands up and in contact with the opponent. What is important to study here are the variations in this posture. The variations will determine the appropriate response. In many cases, this is why techniques may be repeated—that is, moving to one side or the other—even though it might not seem to matter against an opponent's push or clinching position. The first consideration is the arms. The defender's arms might both be inside or both outside the attacker's arms. Or the defender might have one arm on the inside and one on the outside.

The second consideration is the feet. Either the right foot or the left foot might be forward. The position of the defender's arms and feet, together with the pushing or pulling force of the attacker, determines how one responds. For example, if the defender's right foot is forward and the attacker is pushing on the defender's open or left side, it is easy to lift the right leg, as one might see in the sweep and hammer-fist technique from

Saifa. Or, if the attacker is pushing to the other side, the defender's right forward foot or closed side, it might be easier to absorb the push and step back, as one does in the opening of Seipai kata. And we see another variation of this response in this fourth sequence of Seiunchin kata, where the defender merely pivots from the clinch into the initial position with the left arm up and the right arm down.

In this sequence, starting from a clinch (though it may just as easily be done with the attacker grabbing or punching), the defender's arms are on the outside of the attacker's arms, or the defender's right arm is on the outside while his left arm is on the inside. As the attacker pushes on the defender's left side, the defender pivots, bringing his left arm up inside the attacker's arm, and punches down with his right over the attacker's left arm (fig. 4.19). Typically, the block, attack, and avoidance all occur at the same time.

The next techniques—beginning with a step forward into horse stance as the defender's left hand rotates to grab the attacker's arm or head—are often described as a right uppercut followed by *uraken* and a down attack to the opponent's groin. However, if the primary consideration of self-defense in a life-threatening situation is to inflict the most damage, as gruesome as that may sound, then that *bunkai* is not it. What we see over and over again in the *bunkai* of the classical subjects is the implicit admonition to attack the head or neck, the most vulnerable targets.

This fourth sequence from Seiunchin is no exception. While the uppercut may certainly be used as an uppercut, the more important function of this movement and the next is to get the arm up in a position for a downward attack to the head or neck area. As the forearm—not *uraken*—attacks the opponent's neck or collarbone, the primary function of what is seen as a lower-level *(gedan)* attack is to bring the opponent's head down as the defender steps back (fig. 4.20), finishing with a left downward forearm strike to the back of the opponent's head or neck (fig. 4.21), the same finishing strike we see in the second sequence of this kata. This sequence will be repeated on the other side of the kata. And again we should notice that the retreating step is accompanied by an attack, not a block.

FIGURE 4.19. Using the initial technique of the fourth sequence against an opponent's clinch

FIGURE 4.20. After the uppercut, the right arm circles to bring the opponent's head down.

FIGURE 4.21. The "down block" is used to attack the neck.

Fifth Sequence

The fifth and last sequence of Seiunchin kata begins with an arm-folding technique, often referred to as two elbow techniques in cat stance (figs. 4.22–23). This beginning technique is repeated toward the end of the kata, but only after the repetition of the fourth sequence executed to the southeast corner. Again, it is imperative that one understands the structure of a kata in order to make sense of its *bunkai;* that is, sequences are frequently interrupted, and one should be aware of that. The other important point to remember here is that techniques that occur in pairs, such as these "elbow" techniques in Seiunchin, are most often meant to be used together—that is, each pair should be seen as one technique.

Any arm-folding technique is difficult to describe in words, and still photographs don't help an awful lot. The technique begins with a cross-hand wrist grab. However unlikely it may seem for an aggressor to initiate a cross-hand wrist grab, one should keep in mind that the techniques of Goju-ryu are generally done from close range, and that a cross-hand grab is much more likely to be a part of any confrontation that involves grappling. That being said, this cross-hand grab release shares some things in common with the other grab release techniques in this kata: they all begin by dropping the elbow of the arm that is being grabbed with both hands coming to the outside of the attacker's grabbing arm.

In the first instance of these, the defender's right elbow is dropped and the hand is rotated, bringing it to the outside of the attacker's arm and beginning the release of the grab. Then the left arm is brought up along the outside of the attacker's elbow (fig. 4.24), pressing in and rolling over the arm. Without any pause in the execution of the techniques, the defender then drops back into the second cat stance with the left arm pulling back and the right arm pushing the attacker's wrist forward (fig. 4.25).

One uses the cat stance here because a quick knee attack to the opponent's groin may facilitate the application of the subsequent techniques. And, of course, what we find in this particular sequence, a structure that is found repeatedly in the classical subjects, is that the finishing techniques are only shown on the second side or the second time the "elbow" techniques occur, after the repetition of the fourth sequence on the opposite side.

FIGURES 4.22–23. The initial technique of the last sequence of Seiunchin kata

FIGURE 4.24. The beginning of the first elbow technique against a cross-hand grab

FIGURE 4.25. After stepping back into cat stance, the position the attacker is left in. The kata indicates that the knee could also be brought up to attack.

FIGURE 4.26. Downward forearm strike

The finishing techniques are quite a bit easier to see. Once the arm-folding techniques have unbalanced the attacker and the head has been brought down, the rear hand (the right hand in the first instance and the left hand in the second) reaches over to grab the head. This is a controlling technique. Once this is done, the arm-folding control is no longer necessary, so the other arm is raised slightly so that the forearm can be brought down with force on the neck or collarbone of the opponent (figs. 4.26–27).

Then, to finish, both of the defender's hands are brought around the attacker's head in what is often referred to as a *yama uke* or mountain block—again, somewhat of a misnomer since this is not used as a block or receiving technique—and, dropping back into cat stance, the knee is brought up to attack the opponent's face (fig. 4.28).

FIGURE 4.27. Forearm strike to the neck or collarbone

FIGURE 4.28. Dropping back into cat stance to attack with the knee

❀

I didn't know what to expect the first time I went to Okinawa. I had been training traditional Okinawan Goju-ryu and the classical weapons of Matayoshi *kobudo*. I had learned the rituals and the language of a formal karate dojo and had even managed to pick up some Okinawan *hogen* phrases here and there. But like most Americans, I didn't really know very much about the Okinawan people or their culture. I may have heard mention of the Battle of Okinawa, but I didn't know anything about the devastating effect it had had on the island and its people. It was barely mentioned in high school history books.

We might not even have noticed very much on the ground in Okinawa almost four decades after the war—after all, that's time enough for a whole generation to grow up with no direct experience of the war. There had been so much building going on since the last time my teacher, Kimo Wall, had been in Okinawa in the early 1960s that we had trouble finding Matayoshi sensei's house and dojo. Finally we found him at the market where he leases space to local farmers. It was evening and he was sitting outside the office, talking with Kina Seiko and Oshiro Zenei.

Later that week, Matayoshi sensei commandeered a van and took us on a short drive around Okinawa—an island only sixty miles long and ten miles wide. We stopped to visit traditional villages and to see old-style houses, and then stopped by the Shuri Museum.

The museum is located on a hill overlooking Naha. This, we were told by Matayoshi sensei, was where the old Okinawan samurai families lived a hundred years ago. This is also where you can see the famous Shuri-no-mon, the gate of courtesy, where, as legend has it, karate practitioners would meet before deciding where they could secretly train.

Inside the museum, you can see displays of ancient farming tools and fishing implements, like old weather-worn *eaku* and different types of *nunchiyaku* (horse bridles). There are also *tonfa* (grindstone handles) and *sansetsukon* (three-section staffs). There you begin to appreciate the simple but effective use the Okinawans made of common tools—tools that had nothing to do with war and aggression when they were first carved out of wood.

But one of the most interesting displays in the museum is an exhibit showing Okinawa during the years of World War II and in the rebuilding years after it ended. There may not be any swords beaten into plowshares,

FIGURE 4.29. From left: Oshiro Zenei, the author, Matayoshi Shinpo, Kina Seiko, and Matayoshi's brother-in-law, Miyazato

FIGURE 4.30. The author and his wife, Martha, at Shuri gate

but you can see the peacefulness, resourcefulness, and humility of the Okinawan people. Here you can see military uniforms that were made into children's dresses and trousers, and bomb casings that were cut off and turned into pots and pans. The wing sections from crashed fighter planes were dismantled and used for shelters, many of them making up the walls and roofs of the original Heiwa Dori ("peace street") or marketplace in Naha, run by the widows of Okinawan soldiers. Through it all, there is a kind of quiet contradiction between the violence of its martial arts and the courteous, friendly, and peaceful people of Okinawa.

FIGURE 4.31. Matayoshi with some of the farming and fishing tools the Okinawans used as weapons of self-defense

5

四向戦

SHISOCHIN

FIGURE 5.1. The controlling technique and one of the signature moves of the kata

SHISOCHIN KATA, PRACTICED IN SOME Okinawan Goju-ryu dojo immediately after Saifa and in some schools considerably later, is the third of the classical Chinese-based kata in the Kodokan curriculum, and there would seem to be a logical rationale for this. If Saifa demonstrates responses to a same-side (e.g. left-to-right) wrist grab, and Seiunchin deals largely with responses to a cross-hand (e.g. right-to-right) wrist grab, many of the techniques in Shisochin seem to suggest that the defender is responding to an attacker's two-handed grab or choke.

Oral tradition has it that this was a favorite kata of Miyagi Chojun sensei's in his later years, though in what sense we're supposed to understand that isn't clear. Was it because of the performance aspect of the kata, or did it have to do with the perceived applications of the kata techniques? Or was it a casual comment that somehow took on perhaps undeserved significance as it got passed on to later generations? I once asked Matayoshi sensei which karate style he liked best, Shorin-ryu or Goju-ryu, having learned both from an early age. Once he understood the question, posed to him in our pidgin Japanese, he responded in his limited English: "I like Goju." But I was never entirely sure whether or not he thought we were asking for some assurance, some stamp of approval—after all, we had come all the way to Okinawa to practice Goju—or an opinion. And then there was his intonation. I wasn't quite sure, but he seemed to emphasize either "I" or "like" more than "Goju."

In any event, Shisochin, most often translated as "fighting in four directions," derives its name from the four *shotei* or palm striking techniques (fig. 5.2) that occur in the middle of the kata, according to Hokama Tetsuhiro sensei, the noted karate historian, although there are two other techniques in the kata that are repeated four times as well. Some Goju teachers refer to Shisochin as an intermediate-level kata; however, one should be careful not to pigeonhole any particular kata as easier or more difficult, as more important or less important, than another kata. They are all part of a system, each with unique characteristics, each exploring a different theme, each presenting one with different responses to different self-defense scenarios.

Shisochin, then, is a predominately open-hand kata. There are no punches, though there are many forearm strikes, and the *nukite* or *shotei* strikes (at the beginning of the kata), as they are generally known,

certainly characterize the kata for many people. There are some variations in the way the kata is performed in the major schools of Okinawan
Goju-ryu, but most of these are rather small and would not generally
alter *bunkai* much. However, there is also a certain amount of ambiguity
in some of its techniques; this kata in particular illustrates the difficulties
one can encounter in trying to rediscover the applications of kata moves
that have long been lost or without any reliable written records.

For example, one might argue that each of the sequences in Shisochin begins with a response to an attacker's two-handed grab or choke,
and that each of these four responses or grab releases (figs. 5.3–6) is then
continued with the sequence that begins with one of the four characteristic downward open-hand blocks and palm strikes that form the core
(fig. 5.2), beginning the long sequences in the middle of the kata, or finished with the feet-together, head-twisting posture shown both near the
beginning and the end of the kata (fig. 5.15). This is, of course, dependent
on how one sees the structure of the kata, but at the very least it illustrates
the difficulties in any analysis of Shisochin.

FIGURE 5.2. One of the four open-hand postures for which the kata is named

FIGURES 5.3–6. Four two-hand grab release techniques

Shisochin, I would argue, is composed of four application sequences, but like many of the other classical subjects, the techniques of a given sequence are not always sequential—that is, like most of the other kata that show repetition of the opening or controlling techniques, the finishing techniques are generally only shown after the second repetition. This can be especially difficult when trying to analyze a kata, or understand its structure, if the sequence of techniques is long or when the opening techniques are separated from the controlling techniques, not just the finishing techniques. This is particularly the case with the second sequence of Shisochin kata, the middle section, the techniques that are really the signature moves of the kata.

The other difference we see in Shisochin from the two kata that precede it, Saifa and Seiunchin, is that it doesn't begin with an application sequence. Rather, it begins with three open-hand strikes from a double-arm *kamae,* stepping forward in basic stance (fig. 5.7). The first sequence begins after the third of these open-hand strikes. This *"kamae"* position is more akin to the opening hand positions and stances of Sanseiru, Seisan, and Suparinpei, and for good reason.

THE DOUBLE-ARM *KAMAE* POSTURE

Years ago, when I first started training, everything was much more formal than the training I now do with a few senior students in the barn dojo in back of my house. We'd line up according to seniority and kneel and sit in seiza. "Mokuso!" Of course, it was all very precise, with a good deal of ritual, sort of like the Japanese tea ceremony without the teacups.

"Mokuso yamae!"

"Sensei ni, rei!" the senior student would bark out. And, after all the formal bows, the teacher would take over.

"Kiyotsuke ... rei ... yoi," the teacher would say, pausing between commands as the students responded. And then ... we began practicing kata. And here's where I noticed something.

"Kata Saifa ... yoi ... hajime (begin)." Next was Seiunchin. "Yoi ... hajime." And then Shisochin. "Yoi ... kamae ... hajime." There was that

extra word—kamae. We used kamae not in the general sense of "posture" or even as a command—"kamae te"—but in the connotative sense of "ready to fight." We generally understood it as a ready position, but no one ever asked why the other kata (Saifa, Seiunchin, Seipai, and Kururunfa) didn't begin with a kamae or ready position—the others began simply from "yoi," with the hands down at your sides and the feet parallel, shoulder's distance apart.

In Goju-ryu, putting aside Sanchin and Tensho for obvious reasons, there are four classical kata that begin with this double-arm kamae posture and four kata that don't. Each of these four double-arm kamae postures begins with three basic techniques that are repeated. Each of the other four kata begins immediately with a bunkai sequence, sometimes in threes and sometimes not. Why the difference? If all of the kata are part of the same system, wouldn't we expect that they would conform to the same structure or pattern? Well ... unless there is a message in the structure or pattern.

Saifa begins with a self-defense scenario (bunkai) against a same-side wrist grab (opponent's left to defender's right). Seiunchin begins with a

FIGURE 5.7. The double-arm open-hand kamae posture from Shisochin

self-defense scenario (bunkai) against a cross-hand wrist grab (opponent's right to defender's left). Seipai begins with the opponent grabbing one's shoulder or throat or lapel. Each of these kata shows defensive scenarios (bunkai sequences) against grabs or pushes—though there are certainly techniques in each of them that work equally well against punches or other types of attacks—while Kururunfa, it seems to me, shows responses to an opponent's punch. The other four kata, however, show defenses and responses to an altogether different situation—one that begins from a wrestling clinch or, if you will, the posture one sees at the beginning of a judo match or very nearly an Okinawan sumo contest.

It's almost as if there is a flag or label tacked onto the beginning of the kata, stating, "The techniques of this kata begin from a grappling position," and we are meant to apply the entry techniques at least with this in mind.

So, does this change the way we should be looking at the bunkai of these kata, or open up new possibilities? Should we be rethinking the opening "punches" in Seisan and Sanseiru or questioning the nukite or shotei-tsuki techniques at the beginning of Shisochin? Perhaps it has no significance and was merely a meaningless pattern to be imitated. But it's also worth pointing out that in three of these kata—Shisochin, Sanseiru, and Seisan—each seems to have only three bunkai sequences. Were they, in fact, based on a more grappling-oriented martial art—Shuai Jiao (Chinese wrestling), for instance, or Okinawan sumo?

So what is essential to understand about Shisochin kata? Some of the most interesting techniques in the kata, and ones that the kata as a whole seems to be exploring, begin from this double-arm *kamae*. If one assumes this posture as a starting position with a partner adopting the same posture, many of the arm techniques we see in the kata can be used as release moves against this clinch or two-handed grab, particularly the initial techniques of each sequence, and, of course, the three initial *shotei* strikes at the beginning of the kata.

FIGURE 5.8.

FIGURE 5.9.

FIGURE 5.10.

FIGURES 5.8–11. Four release techniques against double-arm grab

First Sequence

Depending on how one interprets the structural clues of Shisochin—whether there are in fact three or four clearly delineated sequences—each sequence begins with both arms being brought up to deal with an attacker's two-handed grab or clinch. In the first of these, the hands are brought over the attacker's arms and then brought down to the sides as the defender steps back into a left-foot-forward front stance (fig. 5.8). This is the Shodokan-Higa method. A variation of this is what is seen in a number of other schools, bringing both hands up to grab the opponent's wrists and then separating the arms.

One of the advantages of the Shodokan version is that initially the opponent's arms are trapped, bending the elbows and bringing the attacker's head forward and down. Additionally, one doesn't have to be all that strong to perform this technique, as opposed to grabbing the wrists and separating the opponent's arms, although one might argue that there are certain advantages to this approach as well. In the next move, if we follow the more conventional approach to the *bunkai* of

FIGURES 5.12–13. Folding the attacker's arm to bring the head down

Shisochin kata, the defender steps forward along the northeast angle as the right arm scoops the attacker's left arm (fig. 5.12), and then, pivoting into a west-facing left-foot-forward front stance, executes an arm-bar (fig. 5.13).

The purpose of the arm-bar is to control the opponent and to bring the opponent's head down into a position where it can be attacked. The next technique looks similar to the previous one, only executed to the left side. The defender's right arm comes over the attacker's arm, and, stepping to the northwest, the left arm is brought up as the right hand reaches to control the attacker's head, and then the left forearm is used to attack the opponent's neck as the defender pivots once again, this time to an east-facing front stance.

This is how one might describe a more conventional interpretation of these first few techniques of Shisochin kata—that is, the conventional arm-bar *bunkai*. However, there are certain drawbacks to this approach. We might question why there is a need to move through so many techniques to attack the opponent's head in the conventional arm-bar interpretation when it seems as though the opponent's head could be attacked with the forearm strike as one steps into the first right-foot-forward front stance to the northeast angle. In other words, why not pivot at that point, grab the attacker's head with the left hand, and attack with the right forearm while pivoting into the west-facing left-foot-forward stance? And that's exactly the point. This is a more realistic interpretation of this series.

In other words, by separating the northeast angle and northwest angle techniques, and not linking them, we have a *bunkai* that is not dependent on utilizing the conventional arm-bar and consequently a lot easier and faster to execute. In this case, the northeast and northwest angle techniques are used as releases (one of four) from the opponent's two-handed grab (fig. 5.9). After pivoting to strike the opponent's neck with the forearm (fig. 5.17)—the bridging or controlling technique—the upper hand grabs the hair or back of the opponent's head, and the lower hand grabs the chin. Then, as the feet are brought together, the lower hand is forcefully thrust up and the upper hand is pulled down and back, twisting the opponent's head (fig. 5.14). Or, alternatively, one might switch after applying the bridging or controlling forearm technique to the longer sequence of the middle section.

This is a much more interesting approach, looking at the structure of the kata based on four entry techniques, two at the beginning of the kata (figs. 5.3–4, and in application figs. 5.8–9) and two more seen in the second half of the kata (figs. 5.5–6, and in application figs. 5.10–11). Each pair is juxtaposed with the first grab release stepping back and the second stepping forward; which technique the defender might employ is dependent on the dynamic of the self-defense scenario and the position of the arms relative to the attacker's grab. In this case, then, the kata is composed of four different release techniques against an opponent's two-handed grab, two very similar bridging or controlling techniques, and two ways to finish—the first being the feet-together head twist, and the second the head twist we see attached to the long sequence in the middle of the kata.

FIGURE 5.14. The beginning position of the finishing head twist

FIGURE 5.15. This final position of the first kata sequence is often interpreted as simultaneous elbow attacks to the front and rear rather than a head twist.

This last position of the first sequence (fig. 5.15)—feet together, right arm and elbow up, left arm in chamber with the elbow thrust back—has caused many to interpret this technique as simultaneous elbow strikes to the front and rear. One of the problems with that sort of interpretation, however, is that there is nothing in the moves that precede it or follow it to suggest that this is what's going on here. It's important to keep in mind that the hands are both open in the preceding move and closed in this final position. As a general rule, this indicates a grab. And, of course, Goju-ryu techniques will always go for the head or neck, the most vulnerable and lethal targets.

The other techniques that seem ambiguous or at least suggest some differences of interpretation are the four angle techniques and pivoting forearm strikes (fig. 5.1), two in the beginning of the kata to the northeast and northwest and two at the end of the kata to the southeast and southwest. The argument one might make for linking these techniques in pairs and utilizing the more conventional arm-bar is based on what we usually encounter in other kata—for example, the four Seiunchin "elbow" techniques. Other than the series of four repetitions we see in Suparinpei, techniques that occur in repetitions of four usually imply that the paired techniques should be treated as part of a single sequence. This may not be the case here, however, since the origins of the individual kata are obscure and certainly in many respects do not conform to the same structural paradigm. So, as indefinite or ambiguous as it may be, it is probably best to leave it to each individual practitioner as to which of these structures seems closest to the original intent of the kata. Structurally, however, the kata seems to suggest that there are four entry or release techniques, a repetition of four controlling or bridging techniques, two on each side, and two finishing techniques or finishing sequences, each shown on both sides.

Second Sequence

The second sequence of techniques is perhaps the most interesting but also the most difficult to explain. Perhaps the easiest way to explain it, for the moment, is to consider these palm-strike and open-hand blocking techniques as initial entry techniques (figs. 5.16, 5.19)—that is, independent of the four grab release techniques—although one should remember that this is the continuation of a sequence that begins from the grappling or *kamae* posture with one of the four grab releases, applying the first of these techniques after one has executed the forward angle stepping technique and pivot into a forearm attack to the opponent's neck (figs. 5.17–18).

Keeping this in mind, then, this second sequence of moves starts with a 180-degree counterclockwise turn into a south-facing front stance with the left arm up and the right arm down (fig. 5.16). In order to see the actual application here, however, it is essential to remember that in the classical subjects of Goju-ryu, in most cases, one doesn't simply turn to face an opponent. Many schools will do just that in trying to find applications for these four open-hand techniques, referring to them as palm strikes to the face of the opponent. If this were the case, however, turning in kata would have no significance—all kata would be done in a straight line.

FIGURE 5.16. This block and attack posture, one of four, begins the long sequence repeated to the east and west at the front of the kata.

FIGURE 5.17. Controlling forearm strike

This is an essential point that one should remember: The turns in kata generally demonstrate stepping off line or, at the very least, changing one's angular relationship to the attacker by pivoting or turning. The easiest way to explain this is to imagine an opponent stepping in from the west with a left punch. By turning, the defender has side-stepped the incoming attack, placing him or herself at a 90-degree angle to the attacker, blocking the attacker's punch with the right arm as it moves down in a semicircular fashion, while the left forearm is brought up under the attacker's chin (fig. 5.19). And this is the case whether we use this technique as an initial entry technique or as a continuation of one of the grab release techniques.

The difficulty one has in seeing this whole sequence, however, is that this opening or receiving technique is separated structurally from both the controlling and finishing techniques that follow it in the sequence. The next technique in the kata is another 180-degree clockwise turn into a north-facing front stance with the right arm up and the left arm down. This is the same technique, but against an opponent stepping in from the west with

FIGURE 5.18. Bringing the left forearm up to begin the second finishing sequence

FIGURE 5.19. The open hand block and attack executed independently

a right punch, or if the defender has pivoted to that side from one of the initial grab release techniques and left forearm controlling technique.

The third technique in the kata is a 90-degree pivoting turn to the west. In form, this technique looks the same as the first technique in this series—a left-foot-forward front stance with the left arm up and the right arm down—only it is facing to the west. From this position, the kata turns again 180 degrees in a clockwise direction into a right-foot-forward front stance with the right arm up and the left arm down. This technique looks the same as the second technique in this series, only it is facing to the east.

The structure here has certainly contributed to the difficulty most people have in deciphering the applications. It can be more easily understood if the first and fourth techniques are done together and the second and third techniques are done together. Then the rest of the sequence—an open-hand block, kick, and elbow—is repeated twice, once to the east and once to the west, with the final finishing technique—a second elbow to the front—only attached to the end of the second sequence. Or, alternatively, as was pointed out in the discussion of the first sequence above, each separate palm-up strike and palm-down block might be employed after one of the initial grab release techniques. However, in either case, the sequence would continue with an open-hand block or controlling technique, kick, and elbow (figs. 5.21–23).

The essential technique in this sequence, if we treat this sequence as independent of the *kamae* posture and two-hand grab release techniques—and what really distinguishes it from the movement we see in most of the other classical Goju-ryu kata—is the movement we see in the spiraling or hyperbolic open-hand techniques of the paired opening moves. The arms move in great arcing semicircles, while the defender rotates or sidesteps the incoming attack.

As the attacker steps in with a left punch, the defender steps to the side and blocks with the right arm, bringing the left arm up to catch the opponent under the chin or alongside the neck (fig. 5.19). Then pivoting 90 degrees, now into a right-foot-forward front stance, the left arm brings the attacker's head down. This is the beginning of the first paired sequence, continuing with the long series of moves—another open-hand block, kick, and elbow attack—moving from west to east along the front of the kata. The second series, which duplicates these moves but moving from east to west along the front of the kata, begins with a right attack as the defender steps to the side, blocking with the left arm while bringing the right arm up to catch the opponent under the chin or alongside the neck (fig. 5.20). In the moves that follow in this sequence, the defender advances toward the attacker, alternately controlling the opponent with the right and then the left hand, and kicks (figs. 5.21–22). The kick is followed by a hooking arm technique (which coincidently looks like an elbow attack) that catches the opponent's head or neck in the crook of the elbow (fig. 5.23).

This sequence is repeated on both sides, to the east and to the west, and then a second "elbow" technique—the left hand controlling the top of the opponent's head and the right hand being brought up to catch the opponent's chin, twisting the head—is applied as the defender pivots to the front or north (fig. 5.24). Of course, alternatively one could still use the elbow or forearm to attack the opponent's neck in either of these sequences, but the elbow or forearm attack is not in itself nearly as lethal as the attack to the head, twisting the neck, which is also more in keeping with the general tenor of the classical subjects and therefore the more likely application.

FIGURE 5.20.

FIGURE 5.21.

FIGURE 5.22.   FIGURE 5.23.

FIGURE 5.24.

FIGURES 5.20–25. *Bunkai* of the second of the long middle sequences of the kata

This ends the sequence for many schools of Goju-ryu, but the Shodokan-Higa dojo again pivots counterclockwise 180 degrees from this point, throwing the opponent onto the left knee of the front stance, facing south (fig. 5.25).

It should be noted that Shisochin shows the possibility of attacking with the forearms at least as much as the *shotei*. The forearm is an extremely powerful weapon, less likely to be injured in a confrontation, and easier to condition through *kote kitae* drills. It's also worth reiterating that the initial technique of this second sequence—what is often described as a rising palm strike with the opposite arm executing a circular down block—can also be executed after the bridging technique (the forearm to the neck of the opponent) in place of the head-twisting technique done in the feet-together posture (fig. 5.18).

Third Sequence

The third sequence—what I would refer to as the beginning of the second half of the kata—is much the same as the first sequence. Again, two techniques dealing with the opponent's two-handed grab or clinch are shown. The first of these begins by pulling back into a cat stance with both hands being brought up (fig. 5.10), instead of over and down as in the first technique of the kata. What differentiates the opening techniques of the first and third sequences is, at least in part, whether the defender's hands are down and brought up inside the attacker's arms or up and on the outside of the attacker's arms. And the use of the cat stance, as elsewhere in the classical kata, implies that a kick may also be employed. The second of the grab releases here is executed by stepping forward, or toward the attacker, into a right-foot-forward front stance with both arms thrust up between the opponent's arms (fig. 5.11).

From there, the defender advances or follows the attacker by moving in, continuing with the same forearm attacks or controlling techniques we see in the first sequence and finishing by bringing the feet together and twisting the neck. How and when these diagonal techniques are applied is dependent on the position of the arms relative to the attacker's arms. The important

FIGURE 5.26. The last posture

point here is to move quickly from the initial grab release technique, whichever that may be, to the controlling forearm attack (fig. 5.1). From there, one need only move to either of the ending techniques. Then the kata finishes with a turn to the right, in the Shodokan-Higa version, into cat stance, with the left hand pressing down and the right hand pushing up (fig. 5.26).

Another instance of ambiguity referred to earlier comes with this posture at the end of the first and third sequences—feet together, knees bent, one arm held in chamber with the fist at the ribs, and the other arm with the elbow up and the fist next to the ear. While this technique may well be the finishing technique attached to the techniques that precede it (figs. 5.27–28)—as I have described it at the end of the first and third sequences—it seems to function equally well as an initial response to a rear bear hug, and there seems to be no way to determine which application is a better fit for the kata or which application was the originally intended *bunkai* other than an analysis of kata structure, which, for some, may be problematic.

If this alternate interpretation is correct, then it could also serve as the initial technique of the second sequence. In that case, the second sequence

FIGURES 5.27–28. Twisting the head

may in fact show two different ways to begin the sequence. Perhaps this is why there are two sets or pairs of the open-hand palm strikes in front stance techniques.

In this alternate application of the end technique, the attacker has pinned the defender's arms by applying a bear hug from the rear. The defender's response is to forcefully thrust one arm up, driving back with the other elbow, while twisting the body slightly, dropping the weight, and thrusting the hips back into the opponent (fig. 5.29). Once the opponent's grasp is released, the defender turns and continues with either of the techniques or sequences that follow this initial move in kata—that is, the circling arm techniques of the second sequence or the turn into cat stance shown in the final position of the kata, taking the opponent's arm up and pushing the opponent's head down into a knee kick (fig. 5.30). This is certainly a plausible interpretation of these techniques.

One should insert a cautionary note here, however. Just because an individual technique seems to work within the context of a strict interpretation

FIGURES 5.29–30. Escaping the hold, turning, and attacking with the knee

of kata, it may not be the correct application; that is, it may not be the original intent of the kata. But that judgment, really a question of understanding the structure of a kata, may best be left to the individual practitioner.

As Toyama sensei leaned over toward me, he held out his arm and gestured, as if I was supposed to pinch the skin of his forearm. When I hesitated, he reached down and picked up one of the hand weights from the floor next to his chair and began to manipulate it, rotating his wrist and twisting his forearm while he talked, moving the weight back and forth, then side to side.

We had taken a bus to Koza City to visit Toyama Zenshu sensei, the founder and head of Shinjikan. My teacher, Kimo Wall sensei, and Toyama sensei had been friends and training partners many years ago when they both had trained in Toguchi sensei's Shoreikan dojo. Toyama sensei lived on a hill overlooking the city with his dojo on the ground floor, one side

FIGURE 5.31. Front row, from left: the author, Toyama sensei, and Paul Gorter; back row: Toyama sensei's students

with an exposed rock wall. The evening class was just ending, and after warm welcomes and introductions, we listened while Toyama sensei and Kimo sensei reminisced about old times.

After a while, Toyama sensei took us out to the side yard where his old cinder-block dojo stood. Inside he had filled the space with a large square structure of interconnecting scaffolding pipes. We marveled at the strangeness of this contraption, but it wasn't immediately clear what we were looking at. Then Toyama sensei laughed and climbed into it. In addition to the vertical and horizontal pipes, there were also pipes on springs coming out at odd angles. Toyama sensei began to move around the inside of the structure, hitting and slamming the pipes with his forearms, blocking and striking and grabbing as he moved from side to side. After this short demonstration, he climbed out and motioned for each of us to try it out.

Later, sitting in Toyama sensei's living room, he pulled out a three-ring binder filled with notes and pictures for a book he said he was working on. My friend Paul and I leafed through the notebook as Toyama sensei and Kimo sensei continued talking about the old days and people they had both known. But before we left—we had to catch the last bus back to

FIGURE 5.32. Toyama sensei's contraption

Naha—Toyama sensei again leaned over toward me, holding out his arm, and gestured for us to pinch the skin of his forearm. His forearms were tremendously strong, and the skin was so tight that it was impossible to pinch.

On the bus trip back to Naha, I thought about Toyama sensei and his strange training contraption. I think it was some time after that visit that I began to see how important and how ubiquitous forearm strikes were in the classical subjects of Goju-ryu. They were everywhere, they were tremendously powerful, and they could be delivered at extremely close range.

6

十八手

SEIPAI

FIGURE 6.1. The opening of Seipai

THERE IS NO SET ORDER to the study of the Goju-ryu classical kata, even in Okinawa, other than beginning with Saifa and ending with Suparinpei. In my own experience, however, Seipai—the name meaning simply "eighteen"—has generally been regarded as the fourth kata in the syllabus of Kaishu kata. It is one of four kata with a numerological name—the others being Seisan, Sanseiru, and Suparinpei. Yet the numbers in these kata names seem to add little to our understanding of the kata themselves—to say that there are eighteen techniques in Seipai is to offer the serious karate *ka* nothing more than a frustrating conundrum that will ultimately yield no more insight into the kata than what was once suggested to me by a seemingly educated practitioner, that I should try doing the kata slowly under the light of a full moon.

Some have suggested that all the numbers—13 (Seisan), 18 (Seipai), 36 (Sanseiru)—are fractions of 108 (Suparinpei), implying that the techniques of the various kata are also somehow derived from Suparinpei. The number 13, however, is obviously not a whole fraction of 108, and I'm not at all sure what decimal points would imply in this sort of equation.

Others have suggested that the names of these kata, and the corresponding numbers, can best be understood in Buddhist numerological symbolism. In this scenario, the number eighteen is broken down into a mathematical equation, three times six: the three standing for "good, bad, and peace;" and the six representing "color, touch, taste, smell, voice, and justice" or "eye, ear, nose, tongue, body, and spirit." By practicing the kata with this in mind, then, the implication is that we can overcome the eighteen worldly desires.

MYSTERY IN THE MARTIAL ARTS

We seem to love mystery. I'm reminded of that best-seller from years ago: All I Really Need to Know I Learned in Kindergarten *by Robert Fulghum. If only it were that simple! We know differently, but it still doesn't stop us from wishing it were so. I remember Fulghum wistfully chiding us to reawaken that sense of wonder we had as children. He reminds us how fascinated we were once, watching the sprouting seed. "Remember the little seed in the Styrofoam cup," Fulghum writes. "The roots go down and the plant goes up and nobody really knows how or why...."[1]*

But am I to believe that modern-day biologists or botanists don't know "how or why" a seed sprouts? This attempt to reawaken a sense of wonder with the world reminds me of the early-nineteenth-century tug-of-war between science and art—a world experiencing the growing pains of the industrial revolution decried by the romantic poets, each on their Rocinante, galumphing off on their quest to find mystery in nature.

A lost cause, you say? According to an article in the Huffington Post, "45 percent of Americans believe in ghosts."² Less than 40 percent think Darwin was right. We may not all be Doubting Thomases, but we love conspiracy theories, whether they're about 9/11 or the assassination of JFK. Heck, we're pretty sure they're hiding something at Roswell, and a sizable number of us are not at all sure we ever landed on the moon. It's almost as if we'd prefer not to know. We love a good mystery. Remember Twilight Zone? It could happen. "There are more things in heaven and earth than are dreamt of in your philosophy," Hamlet tells Horatio. Oh, how true! And how can you argue against any of this if someone chooses to believe? Faith is hard to shake. It has nothing to do with reason and logic. In fact, reason and logic—the cold, hard facts— can be discomfiting. Faith that doesn't have to answer to logic or reason is, on the other hand, comfortable. I don't think Fulghum has much to worry about. I think given the choice, we'd choose ignorance every time.

Take the martial arts, for instance. It's filled with ritual, and we love ritual. Ritual has no rhyme or reason. We get dressed up in strange-looking pajama-like clothes and parade around with colorful patches and belts or sashes that establish rank and position, and we even genuflect. We love to bow. We use words that the novice or outsider doesn't know—a special language only for the initiated. We have special names: soke, shihan, sensei, sempai. We have decorative shrines. We burn incense. And we have faith that all of this is somehow important to our pursuits—that their meaning will be revealed to us in time. But before you know it, we begin to practice all of these things for their own sake. It reminds me of that story by Borges, if I remember correctly, where the tiger comes into the temple and kills someone so often that it is eventually incorporated into the daily rituals of worship. In the sacred training hall, even the practice of kata becomes some sort of mystical experience.

Sometimes it almost seems to me that people need this sense of mystery in their martial arts, that if we attempted to explain the mystery we would somehow incur the wrath of these reborn romantics, these would-be mystics from an earlier age. Still, I'll never understand why the bunkai that some people do doesn't look like the kata that it is supposed to explain. Nor why the bunkai that they practice is not lethal—why the techniques seem to be just a prelude to a sparring match where, of course, all kata technique will be abandoned. Nor why the steps and turns of a technique in kata do not appear in their bunkai. Nor why there is so little talk of principles that reflect an understanding of a system of movement rather than a collection of an infinite number of techniques. Nor why so many bunkai seem to suggest that the attacker will not hit you with the other hand—the one you have not blocked—even though you have left yourself in a vulnerable position. It's a mystery to me.

None of this is very useful, however, if one is simply trying to figure out *bunkai*. What is of note is that the structure of Seipai kata is unique, at least up to this point. It doesn't begin with a repetition of three techniques—neither the beginnings of a *bunkai* sequence repeated three times as in Saifa and Seiunchin, nor the three repetitions of the starting fundamental open-hand *kamae* that one sees in Shisochin. Rather, Seipai begins with a single complete *bunkai* sequence. In all, Seipai shows five *bunkai* sequences, more individual combinations than any of the other classical kata. Each of the sequences also begins with an outside circular arm block or receiving technique. Further, unlike most of the other classical kata, each sequence, except for the fifth and last sequence, is shown in its entirety and in order—that is, beginning with the receiving technique, continuing with the bridging or controlling technique, and ending with the finishing technique. The last sequence shows an initial or receiving technique only on one side, then repeats the controlling or bridging techniques on each side, and then again shows the finishing technique only attached to the second side. The initial receiving techniques seem to work equally well against punches, but the more likely scenario is against an attacker's grab or choke hold—again, a confrontation that begins from close range.

So what is essential to understand about Seipai kata?

First Sequence

The first sequence of Seipai kata—a step back into horse stance as the left arm comes up to trap and fold the attacker's arm (or block a punch) and the right arm comes out to strike the attacker's neck (fig. 6.1)—is similar to the opening techniques of the last sequence in Saifa kata—a sweep and hammer-fist or downward forearm strike (fig. 3.12). One of the differences in the defender's response is the energy of the attacker.

It's important that the defender be sensitive to the force and pressure of the attack, particularly if the technique is executed from a clinch or grappling-like posture. If the attack is fast or very forceful, or the push is toward the closed or front-leg-weighted side, the defender may need to drop back into horse stance, executing the technique we see here in Seipai. If the attack is less forceful or the push is toward the open side or such that the defender can shift his weight to the rear leg, then one is more likely to execute the technique we see in Saifa, sweeping with the front leg and attacking with the downward hammer fist or forearm. In any event, if one is training this technique from a grab or clinch position, it is important to train one's tactile sensitivity, for lack of a better term. We see this a lot in the Chinese martial arts, but it has been sadly lacking in a good deal of karate training.

In the execution of the first technique, bringing the right arm out in a large semicircular motion, what is frequently ignored, perhaps from a misinterpretation of the final position or perhaps simply because the circular motions are in themselves quite beautiful, is the function of the defender's right elbow as the arm is brought up and in. As the left arm is brought down to trap and fold the opponent's arm, the opponent's head is brought in and down. At the same time, the defender's right elbow comes up to attack the opponent's face (fig. 6.2). Then, maintaining contact, the right arm straightens, pushing down on the attacker's neck (fig. 6.3). With the next step forward, the left hand is brought under to the opponent's chin (fig. 6.4). Then, with the left hand on the chin and the right hand on the top of the head, the defender steps forward again (fig. 6.5) and then drops into horse stance, twisting the opponent's neck (fig. 6.6).

FIGURE 6.2.

FIGURE 6.3.

FIGURE 6.4.

FIGURE 6.5

FIGURES 6.2–6. The first sequence of Seipai kata

This first sequence of Seipai kata demonstrates a few of the things we see repeatedly in the Goju classical subjects—the receiving block is often accompanied by a counterattack; the initial response is immediately followed by techniques directed at the opponent's head or neck; and, lastly, the finishing technique used in the classical subjects is generally a head or neck twist, though in many kata we will also see forearm strikes and knee kicks to the head.

Second Sequence

The second sequence begins with a circular block with the left forearm as one steps forward with the left leg, hooking the left foot behind the opponent's right foot (fig. 6.7). This is followed by a right *shuto* attack to the opponent's neck and a right front kick. Then, grabbing the opponent's head, the defender drops back into horse stance, twisting the head and flipping the opponent over, and striking down with the left elbow (figs. 6.8–9). This technique can also be executed against a right punch, a shoulder grab, or a choke.

It is worth noting here that the left blocking arm comes up and across in a clockwise circular motion in both of these first two sequences. In fact, there are a number of similarities in the different sequences, not only in

FIGURE 6.7. The first technique of the second sequence

FIGURES 6.8–9. Final position of the second sequence: a downward elbow attack

this kata but in the other classical subjects as well, such that one begins to notice certain themes. This is an important aspect in the study and practice of kata. I have students who would rather spend all their training time doing *bunkai*—and I understand this feeling. Kata without *bunkai,* after all, is just empty movement. But there is also a lot to be gained by doing kata, and even in watching others do kata. The study of kata, I would argue, can be a better vehicle for understanding the themes of kata. And once we get to this point, it is that much easier to move from one *bunkai* to another, to apply techniques depending on how the opponent moves in a given situation, not according to a prearranged plan or drill.

Third Sequence

The third sequence is also against an attacker's grab or choke hold, probably one of the reasons we don't see very much lateral movement in the defense scenarios of Seipai kata. The defender's hand is brought up on the outside to grab or secure the attacker's right hand, while the defender's right forearm is brought up to strike the inside of the attacker's upper arm, above the elbow (fig. 6.11).

FIGURE 6.10. Controlling the opponent and attacking with the knee

FIGURE 6.11. This receiving technique is harder to see, as the application begins between the end of the last technique and before the next one.

FIGURES 6.12–13. Applying the arm-bar to bring the opponent's head down and pulling back into cat stance in order to use the knee

Then, as the defender pivots into a right-foot-forward front stance to the south, and while the left hand maintains control of the attacker's wrist or hand, the right arm is rolled over the attacker's elbow (fig. 6.12). The purpose of this arm-bar, working against the elbow joint, is to force the attacker's head down, while the defender moves to the outside. Once there, the defender pulls back into cat stance, and the right hand comes up and rotates over to grab the head or hair (fig. 6.13). In ancient times, this would no doubt have been another instance where the topknot was grabbed. Again, as is true in other kata, the cat stance signifies a knee kick, directed in this case at the face.

At this point, the defender steps in with the left foot. Maintaining the hair grab, the left arm is brought up and over the attacker's neck. As the defender turns to the original front direction, the left forearm is brought up across the attacker's throat (fig. 6.14). In the final technique, the neck break, the defender opens the left hand and grabs the attacker's chin, then pivots and steps in a counterclockwise direction, the left hand pulling the chin up as the right hand pushes the top of the head down.

FIGURE 6.14. Attacking the head before turning and twisting the neck

The techniques of this sequence have generally been misunderstood. Instead of bringing the arm around the opponent's head, pulling down on the hair with the right arm and thrusting the left forearm up across the attacker's throat, most teachers show this technique as an arm-bar, a technique that is not at all lethal in this instance and particularly unrealistic—allowing the opponent to strike with the other hand. The defender in this scenario would also be turning his back on the attacker.

I don't know why this sort of interpretation has found such widespread acceptance; perhaps because it is a lot easier and safer to practice. But I suspect that one of the problems is that most instructors do not see the connection between the different techniques in this sequence. Most begin their analysis of the kata movements from the right open-hand block in cat stance (fig. 6.10). They imagine that the attacker is grabbing the right wrist or stepping in with a right punch. They finish the sequence with a right palm strike to the opponent's groin. Again, one of the problems here is that these kinds of techniques are not really finishing techniques—they're not very lethal.

Fourth Sequence

The fourth sequence begins with a step along the diagonal to the southeast corner of the kata, executing a left circular block and right palm strike (fig. 6.15). This is the same block we see in the second sequence, and like that sequence, the attack may be a right punch, a grab, or a choke. It is important to see these similarities, because the kata is essentially showing variations in how one responds to these attacks based on the dynamics of the situation.

In the second sequence of the kata, the defender is "receiving" or responding to the initial attack in the same way but, after the kick, dropping back. In this fourth sequence, the defender is stepping forward or following the attacker. In this sequence, after the initial block and counterattack (figs. 6.16–17), the defender steps forward, past the attacker's right hip, with his right foot. At the same time, the defender's right arm carries the attacker's head around (fig. 6.18) and, grasping it now with both hands, does a hip throw, taking the opponent to the ground. This is all executed, of course, with fluidity—that is, without any gaps or pauses in the execution of any of the techniques. Then, stepping back into horse stance

FIGURE 6.15. The first technique of the fourth sequence

FIGURE 6.16.

and holding onto the opponent's hair with the right hand, the defender delivers a left downward forearm strike to the opponent's neck. The kata repeats this sequence to the other side, along the southwest diagonal.

FIGURE 6.17.

FIGURES 6.16–18. Moving in to throw the opponent

Fifth Sequence

The fifth sequence begins with an off-line step into a left-foot-forward cat stance and a right hooking punch (figs. 6.19–20). Again, this opening technique may be executed against a punch, a grab, or a choke. In the next technique, quite crucial to an understanding of this sequence, the defender pivots, dropping the weight onto the left foot, with both arms brought down on the attacker's arm or arms (fig. 6.21).

The defender then steps forward into a cross-footed stance, behind the attacker, with the left foot coming in back of the right, as both arms are brought up in what appears to be a mirror image of the previous technique (fig. 6.22). In this technique, the defender is coming in to simultaneously attack the opponent's head, striking the neck with the left forearm, and grab with both hands—the right hand grabs the opponent's chin as the left hand controls the head.

Then, pivoting 270 degrees in a counterclockwise direction, finishing in a left-foot-forward basic stance, the defender brings the opponent around,

FIGURES 6.19–20. First technique of the last sequence

twisting the head. From this position, the defender reaches up with the left open hand to grab the attacker's hair or topknot (fig. 6.23), then pivots, bringing the head down (fig. 6.24). The next technique appears to be a downward *uraken* strike, but the purpose here is merely to twist one's grip on the opponent's hair in order to bring the chin up (facing away from the defender), suggesting that the movement has been exaggerated.

In the next technique, pivoting back to the west to face the opponent, the defender reaches over with the right hand to grab the opponent's chin and simultaneously kick with the right leg, the kick or knee helping to bring the chin up. Then, stepping back into horse stance, the defender pushes out with the left hand that has grabbed the hair and pulls back with the right hand that has grabbed the chin, twisting the opponent's neck.

One would, I suppose, expect the sequence to end with this neck twist. Most of the sequences in the Goju-ryu classical kata tend to end with a single neck twist, or at most two neck twisting techniques. If you include the twisting motion contained in the 270-degree turn, this would be the second neck

FIGURE 6.21. Moving from the outside to the inside gate

FIGURE 6.22. Attacking the head

twist. It seems like overkill. But the sequence of kata moves here is fairly clear—that is, it is what it is. Again, when this is done without any gaps or pauses, it is surprisingly fast and completely disorienting for the attacker.

FIGURES 6.23–24. Pulling the attacker's head down from the rear

FIGURE 6.25. Grabbing the head for the final throw

However, the final technique, shown only on the second side, the latter part of the sequence repeated to the west, is also a head twist and throw. In this last technique, the defender steps around the attacker to face the original front of the kata, grabbing the opponent's head in both hands, one hand on the top of the head and one on the chin (fig. 6.25). This is the peculiar cross-footed stance we see at the end of the kata, with one hand over the other, palms facing, at the level of the solar plexus. Then, stepping back into cat stance and striking with the knee, both arms circle to twist the opponent's head and finish with a hammer-fist strike.

Much of this sequence is markedly different from what has traditionally been taught, if it has been taught at all, as the standard *bunkai*. Of course, most interpretations of these techniques do not usually consider all of these techniques to be part of the same sequence. And that is generally the problem—that individual techniques are not seen as part of a whole. It has even been suggested by some teachers that each technique should be able to end an encounter. That in itself presupposes that all the techniques are in essence the same—that one doesn't necessarily need to distinguish between entry techniques, bridging techniques, and finishing techniques. But this also ignores any consideration of kata structure. And while there are general similarities among the various classical subjects, each kata may also exhibit unique structural differences.

In Seipai kata, one of these differences is seen in the last sequence. The middle section of this sequence is repeated on both the right and left sides of the kata. The final techniques are attached only to the second repetition, typical of many Goju-ryu sequences. However, the opening or initial techniques are only shown on the first side of the kata. This is not so typical in the classical subjects. The implication then may be that the techniques on the repeated or second side could be done without the initial receiving technique shown on the first side—that the first technique on the second side could also function as an entry technique given a different scenario.

One of the other places we see this kind of structure is the third sequence of Saifa kata. Whether we interpret the two circular arm techniques followed by kicks as initial entry techniques or as a continuation of the previous sequence, the sequence that follows them, the structure suggests, could function either as finishing techniques or as a complete sequence of its own. And while this may seem an unnecessarily arcane discussion, it is unquestionably important to understand kata structure, at least in a general sense.

Before I ever got on a plane and took that twenty-hour-plus flight to Okinawa, I had heard stories about Matayoshi Shinpo sensei. My teacher, Kimo Wall sensei, had been a young Marine in the early 1960s stationed on Okinawa. He had trained karate since he was six years old, so finding himself in Okinawa, and armed with letters of introduction, he began training in the Shoreikan dojo of Toguchi Seikichi sensei and the Shodokan dojo of Higa Seiko sensei. It was there that he began studying *kobudo* with Matayoshi, who shared the old Shodokan dojo with Higa. And, as luck would have it, since Kimo sensei had a car, he would often run errands for both Matayoshi and Higa, becoming a close friend to both families.

So when I started training *kobudo* with Kimo sensei, we heard a lot of the old stories—how they would fashion their own *rokushaku bo* (six-foot staff) with a glass shard from a broken Coke bottle or how Matayoshi would send them off into the fields to learn how the *kama* (sickle) was really used. I heard stories of Matayoshi's prowess, of how he had learned Shorin-ryu from his father and trained Goju-ryu under Higa Seiko sensei, how he had learned Kingai-ryu, and, of course, the weapons of Okinawa *kobudo*.

Kimo sensei had even told me a story once of how he had been sitting in the dojo one evening, talking with Matayoshi sensei. They were talking about *ki* (or *ch'i* in the Chinese arts) and *kiai* that starts in the *tanden* (or *dantian* in the Chinese arts), energy that is directed by one's spirit and manifested in a loud shout. Among the different forms of *kiai* used in the martial arts, Matayoshi mentioned a silent *kiai*. When Kimo sensei gave him a questioning look, Matayoshi said, "Sure," and turned, looking intently at the cat, asleep by the door. A moment later, the cat jumped up as if startled and bolted out the door. Kimo sensei remembered the incident many years later, convinced that he had witnessed a silent *kiai*.

FIGURE 6.26. The author's wife, Martha, demonstrating for a TV interview of Matayoshi sensei.

I love all the old stories, the stuff of legend, but I'm a bit more skeptical. Most of the great martial artists, at least all the ones I've known, were approachable, humble, and kind people. They just trained really hard. Matayoshi himself often laughed and joked around with us, but he had spent a lifetime training the martial arts. He was tremendously caring and generous, and seemed to be very down-to-earth.

FIGURE 6.27. Matayoshi Shinpo demonstrating Kakuho kata from his family system, Kingai-ryu

One afternoon, a Japanese film crew came to the dojo to do a feature on Matayoshi sensei. The dojo is small, on the ground floor of Matayoshi's house in Naha, and it was filled with students, many, like us, from different parts of the world. The film crew set up a small table and chairs in the corner of the dojo, where a television hostess could interview Sensei. We were all gathered on one side of the dojo, quietly watching everything. And then, Matayoshi sensei was asked to demonstrate a kata. He got up, straightened his *gi* top, walked in his Chaplin-esque fashion over to the far end of the dojo, and bowed. Then something happened that I don't have the words to describe. As soon as he began to move, Matayoshi sensei became something else. His face and manner and movements changed, took on a ferocity that I had never seen there. It was as if he became the tiger or the fighting crane that his movements imitated. I was mesmerized, like everyone else, by his performance. It lasted a minute or a minute and a half, and then it was done. He bowed and laughed as he walked back to his chair. It was over. The interview lasted a few more minutes and then that was done too. But I had seen something. Though I didn't know what it was or even how to describe it, I knew it was something unusual.

7

三十六手

SANSEIRU

FIGURE 7.1. The final position of Sanseiru

SANSEIRU IS THE NEXT KATA we generally practice in the canon of Goju-ryu classical subjects, though this is certainly not a given by any means. Some schools place it earlier, while others place it later in the syllabus. In the Shodokan syllabus, in fact, it is placed just before Suparinpei.

Karate lore suggests that this kata may have been a late addition to Miyagi's Goju, that Higashionna Kanryo sensei had not taught the kata to Miyagi, though it is generally acknowledged that he did teach the kata to Kyoda Juhatsu. It's not clear why this may have been the case, or why, among all of the classical kata of Goju-ryu, Sanseiru seems to show the most variation in its performance. The Higa version differs in places from the versions practiced in the Shoreikan, Meibukan, and Jundokan dojos, as well as the To'on-ryu of Kiyoda Juhatsu. Some of these differences appear to be quite significant, yet at least in some cases, where these differences might seem pronounced, the same *bunkai* can still be found.

The name, Sanseiru, like some of the other kata, refers to a number, in this case, thirty-six, and the same explanations have often been given: either there are thirty-six distinct techniques in the kata—though attempting to actually count the possibilities will no doubt prove to be a frustrating and fruitless endeavor—or this is once again a reference to Buddhist numerology. Neither sheds much light on the practice or the structure of the kata itself, however. More to the point, one should note that the kata begins with three slow "punches" in basic stance, followed by three *bunkai* sequences. The first of these sequences is complete—that is, it has a beginning, a middle, and an ending. The second distinct segment of the kata shows a core sequence that is repeated three times with an ending tacked onto the third repetition. The third distinct segment shows a middle or controlling technique, without a corresponding opening technique, followed by a finishing technique attached to the second repetition. This may indeed seem like a complicated structure for a kata, suggesting that the sequences were intentionally hidden from casual observers. After all, this sort of "conspiracy theory" has long haunted karate lore. And for all anyone knows, it could be true. But the middle or controlling or bridging technique here, call it what you will, comes off the central core technique, and the core entry technique is repeated three times in the kata—just as the *kamae* posture at the beginning of the kata is—and that may have been a clear enough message for anyone who knew the kata.

Sanseiru, like Shisochin and two of the other *bunkai* kata, begins from the *kamae* posture, both arms up, like Sanchin, with the arms bent and the fists at about shoulder level. Again, the *kamae* posture is significant. From *heiko dachi* (feet parallel and shoulder's distance apart), one steps forward into a right-foot-forward basic stance, executing a slow "punch" off the rear leg. This technique is repeated, stepping forward with the left foot, and then once more with the right foot forward, though some schools will execute this last "punch" quickly. However, one should focus on pulling the "punch" back into the *kamae* position at least as much as pushing the "punch" out, as this is an important aspect of the core movements of this kata. It is also important if one is to understand the purpose of beginning in the *kamae* or grappling posture.

Like Shisochin, the opening of Sanseiru is composed of three fundamental techniques that do not show a *bunkai* sequence but instead show an opening position, one similar to the starting clinch posture of a wrestling match, and its repeated presence at the beginning of Goju kata underscores its importance in the practice and analysis of techniques in the classical subjects. Most of the time we tend to practice *ippon kumite* with one student taking on the role of attacker—punching, pushing, grabbing, or choking—and the other taking on the role of the defender who employs kata techniques. The message contained in these *"kamae"* kata—Shisochin, Sanseiru, Seisan, and Suparinpei—suggests that this starting posture, where neither person seems to have a distinct advantage, is worth studying. Furthermore, one will see the advantage of using Sanchin *dachi*, the basic stance, here and why it is so prevalent in Goju. With this posture—both arms up and the weight equally distributed on both feet—it is relatively easy to shift and redirect the opponent's push to either side. It is also relatively easy to step as the opponent's push is redirected or slipped off the front-leg closed side or the rear-leg open side. And in so doing, the fundamental beginning arm techniques in these *"kamae"* kata are used in a variety of ways against the opponent's arms, teaching the defender to be sensitive to the push and pull, the energy, if you will, of the attacker. To those familiar with the Taiji pushing hands exercise, this will seem somewhat familiar.

First Sequence

The first sequence begins from this double *kamae* position (fig. 7.2), though the initial technique we see in this sequence can just as easily be done against an attacker's right hand grab or punch. As the opponent pushes in or attacks with his right hand, the defender grabs the attacker's right wrist or hand with his right hand and controls the attacker's elbow with his left hand (fig. 7.3), stepping back into a left-foot-forward front stance (fig. 7.4 in kata and fig. 7.5 in application). The effect of this—and in fact the whole purpose of the arm bar—is to bring the attacker's head forward and down. Many schools look at the finished position here and assume that the defender is blocking a low front kick. However, the impracticality of that—with the defender's face lowered and in an indefensible position against the attacker's hands—should be obvious.

After gaining control of the opponent with the arm bar, then, the defender steps in with the right foot and grabs the defender's head with the right hand. This is followed with a left knee kick to the opponent's ribs (fig. 7.6). (Some schools will kick with both the left and the right here.) Then, once again stepping forward with the right foot, the defender hooks the opponent's head, coming up under the neck with what looks like an elbow attack, and punches. This is followed by a knee kick or simply a down side-kick to the opponent's knee or side of the leg. The kick, of course, can also be used to throw the opponent as the defender turns.

This is the simplest explanation for this sequence. A more deadly version of this sequence would have the defender grabbing the opponent's hair or topknot—this can be done with either hand after the arm bar—and, with the other hand on the opponent's chin, the "elbow" attack and "punch" becomes a twisting neck break (fig. 7.7).

The description of this part of the *bunkai* sequence may seem somewhat baffling, particularly if one is used to seeing the raised elbow here as an elbow attack or every closed fist attack as a punch. But the elbow attack in Shisochin is used in a similar manner, and one should always remember the oft repeated adage: A punch is not always a punch. In Goju-ryu, where there aren't very many punches to begin with, the "punch" is more often than not something else.

FIGURE 7.2. The beginning *kamae* posture

FIGURE 7.3. The beginning of the first sequence

FIGURES 7.4–5. The first technique—a step back into a low front stance—uses an arm bar to bring the opponent down.

FIGURE 7.6. Maintaining control of the opponent, the knee is used to attack the ribs.

FIGURE 7.7. The elbow technique is used to hook the neck of the opponent or to attack the chin and twist the head.

Second Sequence

The second sequence of Sanseiru begins with a 180-degree counterclockwise turn to the south into a left-foot-forward basic stance with the left arm up in a *chudan uke*—at least this is what the final position of this move looks like. This turn into the middle-level block should remind one of the opening position. Both arms are actually employed on the turn. This initial technique, in fact, illustrates an important point that should be kept in mind wherever we see turns in kata that begin a new sequence. One of the things that hampers our ability to see *bunkai* is that we frequently look for applications in the final positions of techniques—that is, as if we were looking at still photographs. Because karate is movement, techniques often begin before we think they begin. Or, as someone once said rather cryptically, the important stuff happens in between the movements of kata.

What is happening in this case, on the turn, is that the defender is stepping off line to avoid the attacker, who is stepping in from the west. For example, if we imagine the attacker stepping in with a left punch, the defender steps off line to the outside of the attack and blocks it with the right forearm, the arm that is actually closest to the attacker on the turn—and one should note that from the previous position, the arm is brought down and across, though the actual movement is executed more by the turning of the body than the muscles of the arm. Then, almost simultaneously, the defender brings the left arm up to sandwich or scissor the attacker's arm, pulling with the left and pushing forward and down with the right (fig. 7.8). This technique, however, is not held. The defender immediately follows this with a low kick to the attacker's knee. In the rest of the sequence, similar to the end of the first sequence, the right arm comes up to hook around the neck of the attacker, finishing with the punch and kick, just as we see in the first sequence. And, of course, it should be kept in mind that this sequence might just as easily begin from the *kamae* clinch position, though at least initially it may be easier to see what's happening if the attacker begins with a punch, as I have described it here.

This sequence is repeated three times with the ending tacked onto the third repetition. The ending of this sequence shows the defender first

FIGURE 7.8. The block and arm-locking technique is used to turn the opponent and bring the head down.

FIGURES 7.9–10. The x-block is not used to block a kick.

FIGURES 7.11–12. The two x-blocks, one with closed hands and one with open hands, are used to bring the opponent's head down and to attack the head, respectively.

using the right knee kick and then pushing the attacker's head down (the first x-block as shown in figure 7.11), stepping back with the right foot into a second horse stance while dragging the attacker over with the left hand, and attacking the opponent's head and neck with the right hand (the second x-block as shown in figure 7.12). This last attack, of course, might be a simple open-hand attack or a head twist. In the Shodokan version of Sanseiru, the second horse stance is accomplished by moving the right foot 90 degrees in a clockwise direction, toward the front of the kata.

There are many schools that have traditionally interpreted these two double-handed downward techniques in horse stance as cross-hand blocks of an opponent's kicks. For any number of reasons, however, one can see the problem with this sort of interpretation. It largely stems from people seeing lower-level techniques in kata and looking for lower-level applications, rather than seeing the techniques of kata in combination.

Third Sequence

The third sequence of Sanseiru is an incomplete sequence, and consequently has presented the biggest problem for those trying to understand the *bunkai* of this kata. The problem is that it begins with the controlling technique (fig. 7.13). The entry or initial opening technique for this sequence is what we generally refer to as the "core" technique, the double-arm locking position or scissor technique we see both at the start of the kata—the double *kamae* posture—and at the beginning of the second sequence (fig. 7.8). This is the "core" technique here, one of the themes that the kata is exploring, because all of the *bunkai* can be executed from this initial starting position, the initial locking technique on the attacker's arm. Because of the asymmetrical structure of the kata, this technique is only demonstrated on one side, against an opponent's left arm—obviously both sides should be practiced outside simple kata practice—but the controlling techniques of the third sequence are shown on both sides, first as if it is coming off the "core" technique locking the opponent's right arm, and then secondly as if it is coming off the "core" technique locking the opponent's left arm.

FIGURE 7.13. This open hand technique is actually the controlling technique of this final sequence, meant to be attached to the core technique.

BALANCE AND ASYMMETRY IN KATA

It may be useful to digress for a moment to address this notion of symmetry and asymmetry, since it has been a subject that has aroused considerable debate, even prompting comparisons of different kata in an attempt to find some evidence to support theories that the different kata have different origins—that they are not, in fact, each part of a unified system. This, in turn, has sometimes been used to bolster the claims of authenticity of one style or another. Some of the "evidence" relies on a comparison of techniques that occur in the different kata—for instance, some kata end in cat stance and some don't. And some have pointed to the perceived asymmetrical nature of some kata and the symmetrical nature of others.

Of course, all of the Goju-ryu classical subjects are unbalanced and asymmetrical to some extent. The training subjects—balanced on the right and the left and largely symmetrical—are an entirely different case, created in the early 20th century along predetermined patterns and for entirely different purposes. (This would include the Fukyu, Gekisai, Gekiha, and Kakuha kata of Goju-ryu, and the Pinan kata of Shorin-ryu.) The classical subjects, on the other hand, are more organic—their movements and patterns determined by the themes they are exploring and the bunkai they seek to preserve. In fact, once one understands the structures of these kata, the patterns—whether they are seen as symmetrical or asymmetrical—may seem somewhat arbitrary. So the asymmetry may have to do with the fact that the kata is only showing a single sequence, as in the opening techniques of Seipai, against a right-hand attack, or it may have to do with the kata showing both sides of an opening technique with the controlling or finishing technique shown only once, tacked onto the second side. Or, as in Sanseiru kata, it may show the entry technique done only on one side but the controlling technique done on both sides, to the left and the right, and then the finishing technique again shown only once.

Many people have found this sort of asymmetry puzzling. Some have even made a concerted effort to balance kata, to do kata in such a way as to show both sides of each technique. This is fine if it is employed as a training exercise, but it would be easier just to take the individual techniques out of the kata and do them as basics instead of the generic head, chest, and down blocks and punches that usually begin training sessions in most karate schools.

Of course, the question is: Why do we find this asymmetry a problem in the first place? Why does a kata need to be balanced? A kata is not a performance piece. I think too often in modern karate practice we treat our karate— and particularly the execution of kata—as if it were a performance. But kata is, above all else, a repository of technique. It contains the principles and self-defense techniques of the system. To impose an artificial construct of balance on kata is akin to trying to fit the pieces of a chair together with square tenons and round mortises, as the Chinese might say; it just doesn't work. At best it's going to be pretty shaky. Which techniques do you balance? How do you know where to connect the techniques of a sequence unless you know where the original sequence begins and ends, and what was initially "unbalanced" about it?

Questions are important if we are to understand the structure of kata and how the different techniques fit together. But there are more important questions to ask—questions that lead one to a better understanding of a kata's applications. In Sanseiru, for example, it's more important to know why there are three block-kick-elbow techniques in the middle of the kata. Or how the open-hand techniques in the middle of the kata function when so much of the rest of the kata uses the closed hand. It's more important to know how many entry techniques there are or how many finishing techniques. And what about the three "punches" at the beginning of the kata?

These are difficult questions because they have to do with what is essential to an understanding of Sanseiru and its bunkai. They may take years of trial and error and much open-minded thought and experimentation. Perhaps that's why people look for balance, because not having the answers to these questions makes one feel a little unbalanced, a little uncomfortable. But it's not about balance or imbalance, symmetry or asymmetry; it's about understanding the structure.

Being a little uncomfortable can sometimes be a good thing, though, which is why I like Sanseiru kata. It's sort of like that old crab apple tree I used to have alongside the driveway. It had a really long branch coming off the left side, so that it looked a bit unbalanced. But that's the nature of trees, I think, part of their beauty, sort of an organic growth that just happens for one reason or another—mysterious and beautiful at the same time. Sort of like kata.

Once the "core" locking technique is executed, the defender's leading arm—the arm closest to the attacker and on the outside of his arm—comes up to grab the attacker's chin, while the defender's other arm—the arm on the inside the attacker's arm—hooks around in an attack to the head as the defender steps in (fig. 7.14). Then, holding onto the attacker's head with both hands, the defender steps in again, twisting the opponent's head with what looks in kata like a closed-fist double punch (fig. 7.15).

The controlling technique here is what varies in kata in different schools. Some schools perform this technique in horse stance (fig. 7.16) while others perform it in basic stance. Some schools bring the hands and arms across in a more circular fashion, from outside to inside. And some schools bring both arms in, leading with the elbow or forearm of the upper arm and performing what looks like a palm-up *nukite* with the lower hand. The interesting thing is that however it is done, regardless of the differences, the *bunkai* is the same. To me, this is a strong

FIGURES 7.14–15. The lower hand controls the opponent's chin while the upper hand controls the head. Then both hands are rotated and thrust forward, twisting the head. This is the first of the two controlling techniques.

FIGURE 7.16. The initial posture of this sequence varies in some Goju schools, but the *bunkai* is the same.

argument for suggesting that originally there was just one *bunkai,* the same *bunkai,* but that different teachers had different ways of accomplishing it.

The last technique in this sequence, what has come to be a signature move for this kata, is the double-arm bent wrist position in horse stance of the finishing move (fig. 7.1). This move is often demonstrated using a hooking motion with the rear hand to capture the opponent's punch and an attack to the opponent's neck or chin with the front bent wrist. I can only think that this application took hold because most people seem to practice karate as a striking art, with various kinds of blocks and punches. If we back up to the previous technique and examine what happens between the previous move—a double "punch" in basic stance to the east—and this last technique (fig. 7.1), we can see that this technique is the finishing move of this sequence and not at all an independently functioning *bunkai*.

In the next-to-last technique of Sanseiru, the defender has hold of the attacker's chin in the right thrusting hand and the hair or the top of the head in the left hand. Immediately after this head twist, the defender's right arm folds in, bringing the attacker's head with it, while the defender's left hand comes underneath to grab the attacker's chin (figs. 7.17–18).

Then, as the defender steps back into horse stance facing the original front—in the Shodokan version of Sanseiru, the left foot steps back with a quarter turn to the left in a counterclockwise direction—the right hand cupping the top of the attacker's head and the left hand cupping the attacker's chin (fig. 7.19), he or she pulls up forcefully on the chin and pushes down on the top of the head for the final neck break (fig. 7.20). What we find then is that this signature position at the end of the kata is actually not a technique on its own but merely the position one finds oneself in after executing the technique that happens between the more obvious moves of kata.

I don't think I ever got much sleep that first summer we spent in Okinawa. Matayoshi sensei put us up in one of his apartments over the market in downtown Naha not far from Heiwa Dori. We slept on the bare tatami floor, using our clothes rolled up and stuffed into a spare T-shirt for a pillow. The market sounds usually woke us around three or four in the morning. After breakfast, we'd usually train by ourselves in Sensei's dojo. Then, in the afternoon, we'd walk around Naha or Matayoshi sensei would show us the sights—a visit to an old *sai* maker or a trip to meet the governor. One afternoon he took us to pay our respects at Miyagi Chojun's tomb. Another afternoon we put on a demonstration for the teacher's union. There always seemed to be something to do or people to meet in Okinawa. Or, if we didn't have anything going on, we'd drop by Shureido and talk to Mr. Nakasone.

FIGURES 7.17–18. An intermediate move in kata with the left hand, palm up, in the crook of the right elbow.

FIGURES 7.19–20. This is the finish of the final, head-twisting technique. The hands are merely rotated, while stepping back and turning to face the front, as if one were holding a ball.

In the evenings, we would train Goju at Gibo Seiki sensei's dojo or *kobudo* at Matayoshi sensei's. It was a hot and busy summer. After warm-ups and basics, we would take a short break to wring out our *gi* tops and have a cup of cold barley tea. When we finished training, generally around 10 p.m., it was still almost 90 degrees Fahrenheit. It was good training, but I had a lot of questions and, after a few weeks, I asked Matayoshi sensei if I could interview him and talk to him about what it was like to train in the old days.

I was curious about a lot of things that I had only read about or things I had heard about from my teacher, and here I was in Okinawa with a chance to find answers. One evening, over sushi at Matayoshi sensei's house, he showed us a four-hundred-year-old *bo* (staff) that had belonged to his father. It was made of coconut tree wood, very flexible, he said, but it splintered. "No good," Sensei said.

FIGURE 7.21. Matayoshi Shinpo demonstrating *manji sai*

After a few days, Matayoshi sensei found a friend who agreed to translate for us and we sat down. We had a list of questions, but we hoped that Sensei would tell us some stories about training under Miyagi sensei and Higa sensei, learning *kobudo* from his father and studying with Gokenki. Sadly, the translator took over the interview. While he was well-meaning, he knew nothing about the martial arts himself, so had decided to draw up a list of questions and answers ahead of time. There was little room, and perhaps less time, for Sensei to answer any of our questions. What I didn't already know could have been found in almost any biography of Matayoshi sensei or any history of *kobudo* in Okinawa—that he studied *kobudo* from his father, Shorin-ryu from Kyan Chotoku, Goju-ryu from Higa Seiko, and Kingai-ryu from Gokenki. And the personal information seemed trivial—that he liked to swim as a child or that his father employed two jinrickshas or that he had been a top sergeant, or the equivalent, in the Japanese Navy.

FIGURE 7.22. Old house on the streets of Naha

Later, on a long car ride into the countryside, I did ask him about Miyagi Chojun sensei. He told us that Chojun sensei often came to the house to visit his father, and then he turned and pointed out the sugarcane fields along the road. He told us that his ancestor, Gima Shinjo, was credited with promoting the sweet potato on Okinawa.

When I think back now, most of my questions were probably pretty naive. I wish I had asked him about Sanseiru, about why there were so many different versions of the kata. Or why there are three slow "punches" at the beginning of the kata. I suppose I could have asked him about *bunkai* and how they had interpreted kata in the old days. Sometimes, if he was feeling good, he would do little moves here and there from Kingai-ryu kata and then laugh and say, "You no show, OK?" Actually, I think if I had asked about Sanseiru, he might have just laughed and said, "OK, you go play." In other words, "Go practice more, and then maybe you'll find the answers to your questions."

8

十三手

SEISAN

FIGURE 8.1. Attacking with one hand and blocking with the other, from Seisan kata

SEISAN KATA—THE KANJI 十 *(sei)* in the name meaning ten, and 三*(san)* meaning three—is the next kata we generally practice, though in some schools it is taught much earlier. Unlike the other kata names in the Goju-ryu syllabus that reference numbers, the number thirteen here does not necessarily signify any Buddhist concepts, though in Chinese culture it was thought to be a lucky number. This was largely due to a pronunciation of the characters—in Mandarin, thirteen was pronounced *shisan,* and sounded like words that meant "definitely vibrant" or "assured growth." Though whether any of this had to do with the Okinawan pronunciation of the kata is not at all clear. And again, none of this really adds much to our understanding of the kata and its applications. Some, no doubt searching for a more meaningful explanation, have suggested that the thirteen in the kata name implies the number of techniques that can be found in the kata, but almost any count of the techniques that would add up to thirteen would be completely arbitrary and highly selective.

What is apparent is that the kata is composed of three *bunkai* sequences, and that the beginning of the kata, where we find a repetition of fundamental techniques in a number of other classical kata, has three sets of fundamental techniques, each repeated three times, with the last of these techniques followed by a grab and knee or down kick. (Of course, by some reckonings, that would mean the first part of the kata had ten techniques, and the remainder, showing three *bunkai* sequences, added to the first ten would total thirteen!)

The three sequences explore similar themes or techniques that show a common thread, both in comparison with each other and as variations on larger themes common to the other Goju-ryu classical subjects. The purpose of showing the single fundamental techniques at the beginning of the kata—techniques that are not part of an apparent *bunkai* sequence— is not entirely clear. But the fact that there are three sets of fundamental techniques—techniques that appear to be initial or entry techniques rather than bridging or finishing techniques—suggests that they are somehow linked to the three corresponding *bunkai* sequences shown later in the kata. Indeed, each of the techniques we find in the repetition of fundamental techniques at the beginning of the kata, including the two-handed grab and kick, seem to occur in one form or another in each of the three *bunkai* sequences in the remainder of the kata.

Seisan, it should be noted, is also one of what I have referred to as the four classical *kamae* kata, beginning as it does in basic stance with both arms up. Putting these ideas together, one might assume that the three sets of three fundamental techniques, each executed with both arms, show entry techniques that should be practiced along with the *bunkai* sequences—that is, the fundamental techniques at the beginning of the kata show ways of dealing with the grappling or two-handed-grab posture associated with the double *kamae*.

The *bunkai* sequences, as we shall see, also show a kind of entry technique. Each sequence begins with a 90- or 180-degree turn into a circular right-hand intercepting block, followed by a left palm strike (fig. 8.1). This technique can be practiced quite effectively against an opponent stepping in with a left punch. The fact that the individual fundamental techniques at the beginning of the kata are separated from the *bunkai* sequences may suggest that the entry techniques—if in fact they are meant to be seen as entry techniques—are really dependent on how the opponent initiates the attack, whether it is with a punch or from the grappling posture.

BLOCKING IN GOJU-RYU

It may be useful here to look at this possible entry technique—the turn into a circular right-hand intercepting block, followed by a left palm strike—as it is similar to one in Shisochin kata. Both of these techniques utilize the turn in kata to show that the defender is side-stepping the attack, intercepting the attacking arm, redirecting it, and ending in a stance that places the defender at a right angle or 90 degrees to the attacker. In the case of Shisochin, the left forearm is brought up, below the attacker's chin or alongside the neck in a semicircular attack. In Seisan, the left palm strikes straight out to the opponent's face. This is a significant difference as far as the bunkai goes, but the blocking or receiving arm is the same. In that sense, it's all about change— that is, the inevitability of change, yielding to the incoming force.

In Goju-ryu, we see this yielding everywhere. It often reminds me of nature. Whenever I take a walk in the woods, looking at the changes of spring or fall, I'm reminded of how everything yields and changes. Sometimes

I wonder whether the same thought may have occurred to Miyagi Chojun sensei, walking about the countryside or along the shore near Naha. When I look at the "Hakku Kempo," it seems to me to be all about change: Mi wa toki ni shitagai hen ni ozu. (Act in accordance with time and change.) Even when it talks about the breath, it's really about change: Ho wa goju wo tondo su. (The way of breathing is hard and soft.) Or when it makes these wonderfully inclusive analogies between each person and the universe: Ketsumyaku wa nichigetsu ni nitari. (The blood and veins are like the sun and the moon.) Jin shin wa ten chi ni onaji. (Hearts and minds are like the universe ... and the universe is constantly changing.)

Goju-ryu, after all, is the "hard-soft" style. It's soft when it yields, and it yields when the opponent is attacking. When my opponent moves in, I move back or to the side. Or, as the Hakku says, Shin tai wa hakarite riho su. (The feet advance and retreat, separate and meet.) Look at the "blocks" or receiving techniques and you will see that they are generally circular, allowing the defender to redirect the attacker's force or energy rather than to meet it head on. You see this in all of the Goju blocking techniques. I always liked the way my teacher would explain the fourth law—Mi wa toki ni shitagai hen ni ozu. "Meet any situation without difficulty," he would say—a good thing to remember whether you're practicing bunkai or merely practicing life. It's all about change. Or, as the Buddha said, "Everything changes, nothing remains without change."

This technique from Seisan is a good example of this. In this technique, the defender yields by stepping to the side. This is what the first turn in the kata is meant to teach. The defender is not turning 180 degrees to face an attack head on. As the defender turns, the right arm is brought up to contact the attacker's left arm, and then, maintaining contact, the arm is brought down and out. At the same time, the left palm is thrust out, attacking the opponent's face, but the energy for this strike, and the effectiveness of the block, comes largely from the turn. It's all sort of effortless because of yielding and sticking and turning the body. And that's really the important part of understanding how change and yielding applies to the martial arts. That is, when you face someone in Goju, it shouldn't look like two bulls facing off in a field, snorting and pawing the ground, or like two trains headed down the same track from opposite directions. And yet that's often what we see in a lot of bunkai or two-person sets, when one person attempts to overpower another person with brute force rather than technique based on correct principles. We should really try to change all that.

So what are the essential techniques of Seisan?

One might argue that the fundamental techniques at the beginning of the kata are really the essential techniques here, since it might seem as though they appear in one form or another in the subsequent *bunkai* sequences. However, what seems more likely is that each of these beginning techniques is a different way of dealing with the grappling posture that the double *kamae* position calls to mind, and that the three subsequent *bunkai* sequences are meant to be applied after one has dealt with the opponent's grapple. The first of these techniques is a middle-level punch accompanied by a mid-level block (fig. 8.2). The second technique is, variously, depending on which school of Goju one follows, an open-hand "sun and moon" block or a rising palm strike executed with a dropping forearm block (fig. 8.3). The third technique is a knee kick accompanied by a shift forward with a palm-up–palm-down pressing block (fig. 8.4). At the end of this string of fundamental techniques is a two-handed grab and down side-kick.

First Sequence

The first actual complete sequence begins with a 180-degree counterclockwise turn into a left-foot-forward basic stance with the right arm blocking and the left palm striking (fig. 8.5). If we imagine, for the moment, that this is the entry technique of this sequence—that is, if we are not utilizing one of the fundamental techniques shown at the beginning of the kata—then the attacker is stepping in from the west with a left punch. This is the easiest way to visualize, and also to describe, how this sequence begins, because whether we utilize any of the initial grappling openings or not, this is the next technique in the sequence.

FIGURES 8.2–4. The three fundamental opening techniques from the beginning of Seisan kata

FIGURE 8.5. The opening block and attack of Seisan kata

FIGURES 8.6–7. Moving to the outside to control the attacker

After this initial block and attack, the defender's left hand sweeps down along the attacker's left arm, maintaining contact so as to prevent the opponent from attacking with the elbow or turning into the defender, while stepping forward in a right-foot-forward basic stance.

At the same time, the defender's right hand comes up to grab the opponent by the hair (or the topknot in ancient times) or the back of the head (figs. 8.6–7). One should note that the turning over of the hand here—from palm up to rotating the palm forward while the elbow is kept down—is the same movement that we find in the first sequence of Seiunchin kata.

Then, the defender steps forward again, bringing the left hand up to grab the attacker's chin as the right hand pulls down (figs. 8.8–9). (These two stepping techniques are repeated two more times in kata in some schools but not in the Shodokan-Higa lineage.) From this position, holding the attacker's head with both hands, the defender brings the chin in with the left hand (fig. 8.10) and pivots to the west into a right-foot-forward basic stance.

FIGURES 8.8–9. Moving in to attack the head

FIGURE 8.10. The head is twisted prior to turning and snapping the neck.

The finishing techniques are performed to the west. When the kata is performed, these techniques look like two punches followed by a down block and a down side kick. In the *bunkai* sequence, however, the first "punch" twists the attacker's neck, while the second "punch" is used to come up alongside the head and bring it down into an attack with the right knee *(hiza geri)*.

What is of particular interest here is that these techniques are repeated with some variation in the remaining two sequences of the kata. How the sequences vary is worth noting because the variations illustrate how one might apply the techniques under slightly different circumstances or as the situation changes. One should also remember that the rhythm and speed at which applications are executed may vary considerably from kata performance. There should be no gaps or pauses in the execution of *bunkai*.

Second Sequence

The second sequence begins, once again, with a turn into a left-foot-forward basic stance with a right circular arm block and a left palm strike to the attacker's face (as we see in fig. 8.5). And as before, the turn illustrates how one is meant to step off-line, yielding and redirecting the opponent's attack, while at the same time counterattacking.

After this initial block and counterattack, the defender advances, shifting forward into a left-foot-forward horse stance (fig. 8.11). This is the controlling or bridging technique in this sequence. It may be done in a similar fashion to the bridging technique of the first sequence. That is, as the defender drops into horse stance and slides forward, the left arm drops down along the attacker's left arm, pressing forward while maintaining contact. This is important, since it not only serves to safeguard against the attacker's elbow, but helps to turn the attacker. Then, as in the first sequence, the right hand comes forward to grab the hair, and the left hand reaches out for the attacker's chin. When the right "punch" is thrust out, the left hand pulls the attacker's chin back. With the left or second "punch," the chin is thrust out and the neck is twisted forcefully. The third "punch," executed with the right hand, is thrust out and down to bring the opponent's head into the right knee kick. This is where we see the first sequence ending.

FIGURE 8.11. Sliding forward in horse stance

There is also another manner of executing a bridging technique here that I should mention. The kata movements alone aren't clear as to which of these might be preferable; each has certain advantages. In this second method, after the initial block and counterattack, the defender maintains contact with the attacker's left arm, bringing it up and over, as it is transferred to the defender's left arm, while the defender drops under it, shifting forward into a horse stance (figs. 8.12–13).

With this technique, one should see the "sun and moon" block—the second of the three fundamental techniques at the beginning of the Shodokan version of Seisan. Both of the defender's arms are moving in a counterclockwise circle. This is an effective way to move to a position of relative safety behind or to the side of the attacker, though it would seem to be somewhat slower to execute than the other method. What follows, then, is two right punches—the second punch coming up to bring the attacker's head down into the right knee kick, as described above.

The sequence ends, in either case, regardless of which bridging techniques are used, with an additional attack to the opponent's head, a

FIGURES 8.12–13. The alternative technique of shifting forward, dropping under the opponent's arm

head twist, and another knee kick. As one can see from these additional moves tacked onto the second sequence, the level of violence has escalated, so much so that some might see it as overkill. However, one should remember that *bunkai* is an analysis of what's going on in kata, not a judgment of its ethics or its effectiveness. While we can, I would argue, figure out what's going on in kata, we can't really determine why the original creators of kata decided to put the combinations of techniques together in the way they did.

However, it is interesting to note here that what looks like a short punch to the chest (fig. 8.14)—a technique that occurs in a number of kata in different styles of Okinawan karate—is, in each case, probably not a chest punch at all. In each case that I've seen, it's much more likely when we look at the whole sequence of techniques that the defender has managed to bring the attacker's head down, seized it with both hands, and then twisted the head, breaking the neck. This is really what the final position looks like.

FIGURE 8.14. The "short punch" is used to twist the head.

Third Sequence

FIGURE 8.15. In this next-to-last position, the opponent's head is in the left hand, against the right shoulder.

The third sequence again begins with a 180-degree counterclockwise turn into a left-foot-forward basic stance with the right circular arm block and the left palm strike (fig. 8.6). As we see in the two previous sequences, the turn illustrates off-line movement. Both the off-line stepping pattern and the simultaneous block and counterattack are common principles in Goju-ryu.

After the initial block and counter, just as we see in the first two sequences, the defender's left arm sweeps down along the attacker's left arm as the right hand is brought up to grab the hair or the back of the attacker's head. The defender's left arm continues in a clockwise circular direction, coming up to grab the opponent's neck or chin (fig. 8.16). The opponent's head is then pulled into the body (fig. 8.17). These are the controlling or bridging techniques of the sequence. They are somewhat different from the first two sequences since they show no forward movement. Most of the third sequence, in fact, is done in place.

FIGURES 8.16–17. Grabbing the head

The rest of the sequence shows the finishing techniques—a "punch," head twist, and knee kick. These again are techniques we see in the other two sequences of Seisan kata. The "punch" here is the first of two head twists or neck breaks. After the kick—whether a front kick or knee kick is employed to unbalance the opponent—the right fist, holding the head or topknot, is thrust forcefully forward and down, while the left hand, holding the chin or neck, is brought over to the defender's right shoulder (fig. 8.15, as it appears in kata). Then the hands change—the right hand grabbing the attacker's chin with the left hand holding the top of the attacker's head—and, dropping into a cat stance, the defender executes a *mawashi* technique to twist the head and attack once more with the knee kick (figs. 8.18–19).

Many of the techniques in this sequence, as in the other sequences of this kata, have been interpreted in other ways. For example, the controlling technique of this sequence—the grabbing technique that occurs after the initial block and counter—has often been referred to as a lapel grab. It is certainly safer to practice a lapel grab with one's partner as opposed to a head grab, but the defender is then left in the unrealistic position of having both his hands occupied while the opponent is free to counter with either hand. In that scenario, the defender has not really moved in such a way as to allow the attacker only the one initial attack, one of the principles of Okinawan karate, and one that should be kept in mind when analyzing kata. So many of the alternative examples of *bunkai* one encounters share this unrealistic quality. One should always remember that while we can change *bunkai* for a less violent time—as many seem to have done, which is certainly preferable to changing kata—the techniques of Goju-ryu were not originally intended for point competitions or for show; they were meant for self-defense, techniques developed to save one's life in life-threatening confrontations.

FIGURES 8.18–19. The *mawashi* in cat stance is used as a head-twisting technique with a final knee attack.

That morning, after we had stopped by the market office to see Okusan and Kiyomi, Matayoshi sensei's wife and daughter, we headed up to Sensei's dojo. We usually trained for an hour or so in the mornings, before it got really hot. Sometimes Matayoshi sensei would slip his shoes off and come in or just stop by for a minute to say hello and give us letters from home. This morning he watched us do kata.

"*Yukkuri,*" he said. We tried to slow down and do each move as carefully as we could. There had been changes to the way we did kata, and we were trying to adapt to the changes. They began Kururunfa to the right instead of the left in Gibo sensei's dojo, and Sanseiru was very different. Matayoshi sensei watched, offered suggestions here and there, and then, after watching Suparinpei, said, "*Scosi mo' renshu, OK?*" in his own mix of Japanese and English.

After we finished and changed into street clothes, Sensei asked, "Where go now?" We told him that we had planned to go up to Koza to see more dojo. Matayoshi sensei suggested his brother-in-law drive us up.

When we got there, we stopped by the Shoreikan dojo of Toguchi sensei, but it was closed. Then we picked up a watermelon and headed over to Masanobu Shinjo sensei's Shobukan dojo. Masanobu sensei met us at the door. I had seen videos of him doing kata and heard stories of how strong he was. He was short, maybe 5-foot-8 or so, but his arms and hands looked tremendously powerful. While he and Kimo sensei talked, he showed us a video of a trip he took to China with a half dozen of his students. But he said he couldn't find any roots or anything that looked like Okinawan Goju there. It was all gone, he said.

That evening after we got back, we stopped by and invited Matayoshi sensei to join us for dinner—we were headed over to "Ni Kai," the little second-floor eating place on Heiwa Dori where we often went for meals. After we had eaten, over a fresh pot of green tea, conversation turned to karate and *kobudo,* as it usually did. He told us the story of how he had taught the director of *The Karate Kid* one of the White Crane forms of Kingai-ryu, but he didn't want his name in the credits. It was an interesting story. When I think back to that summer, us with our few words of

Japanese and Matayoshi sensei with a smattering of English, I'm often surprised at the conversations we were able to have.

On the walk back to the apartment building, he told us to get our cameras and head up to his house. When we got there, Matayoshi sensei was sitting on the floor amidst a number of Chinese and Japanese scrolls, some old and some new. A lot of them he had received from people who visited him. Some things he had displayed around the room. Other things, like some of these inexpensive scrolls, he rolled up and stored in the closet. At one point he brought out a beautiful raku ware tea bowl and passed it around. Then he unrolled a scroll with a picture of a crane on it. It was a nice drawing but it didn't look like anything special—the kind you might pick up for a few dollars in almost any Asian gift shop. Matayoshi sensei looked over at us and said, "You like? Maybe *janken*, huh?" When we

FIGURE 8.20. The author (right) with Masanobu Shinjo sensei

looked puzzled, he shot out his hand and made the universal motions for rock, paper, scissors. *"Ichi, ni, san,"* and Paul's rock covered my scissors, but I was really not paying attention. Looking at the examples of calligraphy around me, I was reminded of something Toyama Zenshu sensei had said to us, that karate was like calligraphy; there was no wasted movement. Then Toyama sensei picked up a beautiful example of calligraphy on rice paper and, turning it over, pointed out that it could be read on both sides, like kata.

FIGURE 8.21. Matayoshi examining scrolls in his living room one evening

9

久留頓破

KURURUNFA

FIGURE 9.1. The initial technique of the second sequence

KURURUNFA KATA IS GENERALLY REGARDED as an advanced kata, most often placed just before Suparinpei in the canon of Goju-ryu classical subjects. The kanji for Kururunfa, 久留頓破, has been variously translated as "holding on long and striking suddenly" or "forever stops, peacefulness, and tearing" or the even more cryptic and wonderfully poetic "the calm before the storm." None, as might be expected, seem to shed any light on the techniques of the kata, prompting some to suggest that the kata was named after its creator or after a famous general. Kururunfa is said to be one of the kata that Higashionna Kanryo sensei brought back from China, and, if that is indeed the case, then how the Okinawans may have transliterated the Chinese name for the kata may also be an important consideration here, or may have obscured the original meaning of the name altogether.

In any case, the structure of Kururunfa exhibits some unique characteristics. The kata is composed of four *bunkai* sequences. The first sequence is shown on both the right and left sides, but its initial techniques are separated from the controlling and finishing techniques that follow them. The second and third sequences are also shown on both the left and right sides, but in this case they are fairly complete and balanced, with the final finishing technique—the *mawashi* in cat stance in the second sequence and the throw in horse stance in the third sequence—only shown after

FIGURE 9.2. Palm-up–palm-down technique from the first sequence

the second repetition, as is often the case with the classical subjects. And finally, the fourth sequence, structurally different from the other sequences of the kata, is shown only on one side.

But the real variation in kata structure—a structure that we don't see in any of the other classical subjects—occurs with the opening moves, the first sequence. This sequence is done on both the right and left sides, but it is followed by three separate techniques (fig. 9.2). Outside of a single instance of three *mawashi* techniques in the middle of Suparinpei, the repetition of three distinct techniques is really only used at the very beginning of Goju-ryu kata. So what we see here in Kururunfa is a fairly unique structure. The implication is that these are finishing techniques—the first two of which are meant to be attached to each of the right and left side opening techniques. The third repetition of these techniques suggests that it may be used independently of the initial opening techniques; that is, in certain circumstances, beginning from the grappling position, for instance, this palm-up–palm-down technique with its pivoting and hand-changing positions could be used as a release, a bridge to control the head, and a finishing attack to the opponent's head.

NEKO ASHI, THE CAT STANCE

It may be useful to look at the cat stance for a moment, since the cat stance begins the first two sequences in Kururunfa (fig. 9.3). The purpose of the cat stance is to shift the weight onto one leg in order to facilitate the use of the front leg to kick. In that sense, it should not be looked at as a stance one assumes or as a defensive posture.

I have a frisky orange cat that looks as though she has a bit of Maine coon cat in her. I used to have a tabby that would sit on the counter and watch the birds all day. If I happened to walk by, he would jump on my shoulder. The funny thing is that I've never seen either one of them assume a "cat stance."

Now, I know that this is only meant to be a figurative description, as many of the names of martial techniques seem to be, but sometimes I wonder whether this tendency toward poetic descriptions of techniques confuses more than it explains. One person I came across said that "just as the name suggests, the animal form is the cat, and the practitioner should keep in mind the nature of the cat when using this stance." But what is the "nature of the cat"? Another person said that the cat stance was "designed for pivoting, night walking, returning to the rear, blocking, and weapons fighting."

I think there are two things going on here. In one sense, when you give a name to techniques—the more picturesque the better—the techniques are easier to remember, but it also provides a shortcut for training; that is, you can just refer to the name of the technique you want people to practice. It's a lot easier to say "Go practice Single Whip" than it is to tell someone to practice the ninth technique in the form, to borrow some poetically cryptic phrases from Taiji. But does calling a technique "embrace tiger and return to the mountain" really shed light on the technique? Do you really "repulse a monkey" that way? And what would it mean to tell someone to "keep in mind the nature of the mountain"? All of these phrases are needlessly cryptic, it seems to me, and no more useful than telling someone they should "keep in mind the nature of the cat."

The temptation to translate cryptic or figurative language literally is under-standable. We are looking for meaning where meaning is not clear. And so when we see pivoting from a cat stance in Seipai kata, we say cat stance is "designed for pivoting." When we see a step back into cat stance in Seiunchin kata, for example, we say that the cat stance is for "returning to the rear." When we see a cat stance accompanied by a block in Kururunfa kata, we say that the cat stance is "designed for ... blocking."

But what's missing is a more complete understanding of kata and bunkai. As someone perhaps with a little more experience or understanding suggested in the same conversation: "Stances are actually more about shifting position and body weight. In other words, they are not static positions that we assume." When we name and codify techniques—and this is certainly true of stances as well—we make it easier to teach, but we may also be leaving things open to all manner of misinterpretations. Stepping back into "cat stance" at the end of Seiunchin is not so much assuming a particular stance as it is shifting the weight onto the rear leg and off the front leg in order to attack the head (which the defender—using yama uke—has in both hands) by raising the knee sharply into the opponent's face. Blocking in cat stance at the beginning of Kururunfa kata is not so much assuming a particular stance as it is stepping off line and shifting the weight in order to kick. We block the opponent's attack and kick to the opponent's knee, or raise the knee into the attacker's stomach. The diagonal sequences near the beginning of Kururunfa show good examples of high-low attacks. And we don't assume the cat stance and then kick—this is too slow. As soon as we can shift

FIGURE 9.3. Cat stance and block that begins the first sequence of Kururunfa kata

the weight, we kick. The whole point of shifting the weight is to kick—whether with the knee or the foot—not to assume a cat stance.

I can remember hearing criticism about different schools. People would say, "Oh, their cat stances are too low," "Their cat stances are too high," or "In that style, they turn their knees in a little in cat stance in order to protect the groin." But all of this makes sense only if you sit in the cat stance as if it were a ready posture waiting for an attack. It's not, despite what we see in movies like The Karate Kid. Most stances in Goju-ryu are transitional and used in attacking the opponent in various ways. Of course, if you want to merely assume a stance, there's always basic stance.

So what is essential to an understanding of Kururunfa kata?

First Sequence

The first sequence of Kururunfa begins with one of the other ambiguous techniques in the Goju-ryu classical subjects. It isn't at all clear, from the movements of the kata alone, what attack the defender is responding to. In most cases this makes little difference; whether the attack is a grab or a punch doesn't seem to affect how the techniques in most of the kata are applied. In this case, however, particularly if one is strictly following kata movement, the opening technique (fig. 9.3) may be applied in a number of different ways.

For example, if the opponent is attacking with a right punch, both arms are brought up to the outside of the attacker's arm (fig. 9.4). As the defender shifts back into a right-foot-forward cat stance, the weight dropping onto the left foot in order to kick with the right, the right hand grabs the attacker's wrist as the left hand grabs the attacker's elbow. This is immediately followed by a right down-side kick to the side of the opponent's knee (fig. 9.5).

Alternatively, if the opponent is grabbing with his right arm—or if we start from the two-arm grappling position—the defender's left arm is brought over the attacker's arm, folding the arm and bringing the attacker's head into the defender's right forearm as it is brought up and then down across the side of the attacker's neck (fig. 9.6).

In either case, this technique is immediately followed by a down-side kick or knee kick to the attacker's abdomen. The kick, rather than being an end in

FIGURE 9.4. The first technique begins with a step back and to the side, shifting the weight onto the left foot.

FIGURE 9.5. The first technique against a punch with a down side kick

FIGURE 9.6. The first technique against the opponent's clinch

FIGURE 9.7. Moving into the first of the palm-up–palm-down techniques

FIGURE 9.8. Bringing the head down (reverse angle)

itself, is used to disrupt the opponent's balance and bring the head down. The moves that follow the kick are used to control and attack the head, either to drive the palm heel into the back of the head and neck (fig. 9.10) or to twist the head and break the neck (figs. 9.7–8). Again, there is a certain amount of ambiguity here even if one applies a strict interpretation of kata movement. One might argue that any application that shows a twisting of the head is more in line with the other Goju-ryu kata, as finishing techniques that show this seem to be more prevalent. However, there are certainly some finishing techniques in the classical kata that show strikes to the head or neck.

Another variation executed from the grappling position and the arm-folding technique, and somewhat less violent, would have the defender pick up the attacker's right arm with his or her left hand at the opponent's elbow, while stepping forward, and at the same time bringing the opponent's head down with the right arm (fig. 9.9) after the attack to the opponent's neck. Pivoting to the right and twisting or flipping the opponent over, the defender then pivots back to the front and attacks with a downward palm strike (fig. 9.10).

FIGURE 9.9. Picking up the arm and pushing down the head in order to flip the opponent

FIGURES 9.10–11. Pivoting back to the front to attack the head or twist the neck

Second Sequence

The second sequence, balanced on the left and right diagonals for the most part, is less ambiguous. It begins with a drop into a left-foot-forward cat stance facing northwest (figs. 9.1 and 9.12). The opponent is stepping in from the original front direction (north) with a left attack. It doesn't matter in this case whether the attack is a punch or whether the attacker is grabbing or otherwise impeding the defender's left arm. And, as has been noted elsewhere, the angular stepping pattern used here is meant to illustrate off-line movement.

It is interesting to note here that the angular movement—in this case putting the defender in less than a 90-degree angle in relation to the incoming attack—also facilitates the defender's forward movement in the subsequent techniques of this sequence. With the defender moving to a defensive angle, it makes it more difficult for the attacker to retreat as the defender begins to move forward. And as the cat stance suggests, the initial block may be accompanied by a low front kick to the opponent's knee.

With the next technique in the sequence, the defender shifts forward into a left-foot-forward basic stance while parrying or pushing down the attacker's left arm, following this with a left uppercut or forearm attack to the opponent's neck on the attacker's right side (figs. 9.13 and 9.17). Then, as the defender grabs the back of the opponent's head or topknot (fig. 9.14), he kicks to the right or rear knee (figs. 9.15 and 9.18) and brings the right hand up into the opponent's chin (fig. 9.19), carrying it around into the right-foot-forward horse stance (figs. 9.16 and 9.20). The sequence finishes with a step back into cat stance, both hands holding the opponent's head (fig. 9.21). The first of these diagonal sequences—one to the northwest corner and one to the northeast corner—finishes here with this first head twist. However, the final head-twisting technique is only shown after the second of these sequences, when the defender pivots to the original front direction with a *mawashi* technique. This final head-twisting technique is in cat stance, using the knee to attack the head.

A more simplified variation of this *bunkai* would utilize the right elbow or forearm attack as just that, an elbow or forearm attack to the opponent's neck. In this case, after the left uppercut, the defender grabs the head or shoulder of the attacker, kicks to the attacker's right leg, and steps into the right-foot-forward horse stance to attack the neck. Then, stepping back into

FIGURE 9.12. Dropping back to block to begin the second sequence

FIGURE 9.13.   FIGURE 9.14.

FIGURE 9.15.

FIGURES 9.13–16. The second kata sequence from the upper cut

a left foot forward cat stance, the defender brings the opponent's head back with the left hand across the top of the head and the right hand under the attacker's chin. Again, what is not shown on the first side of this sequence is the final head-twisting *mawashi* technique. What should be apparent, however, is that both of these *bunkai* are essentially the same.

FIGURE 9.17.

FIGURE 9.18.

FIGURE 9.19.

FIGURE 9.20.

FIGURES 9.17–21. The second sequence continues, advancing with an upper cut, a kick, and a palm strike to the chin in order to bring the head around. To finish the sequence, the defender steps back into cat stance and twists the head with the *mawashi* technique.

Third Sequence

The third sequence begins with a middle-level palm-up block in basic stance (fig. 9.22). This in itself is an interesting opening or entry technique, especially thematically, since each of the sequences in Kururunfa may be executed from this first technique. And again, this initial technique may be executed from the grappling position or a single punch.

In this case, however, after the initial palm-up block on the outside of the attacker's arm (fig. 9.23), the defender steps in toward the attacker, being careful to protect against the opponent's elbow (fig. 9.24), then pivots to grab the attacker's arm at the wrist while attacking with the right elbow (fig. 9.25).

FIGURE 9.22. The first technique of the third sequence

FIGURE 9.23.   FIGURE 9.24.

FIGURES 9.23–25. The initial block, guard, and attack of the third sequence

The rest of this third sequence is shown on the second side. The defender steps into a right-foot-forward basic stance with the same initial technique, in this case a right middle-level palm-up block. In this second instance, the defender steps toward the attacker, pivoting to grab the arm at the wrist while attacking with the left elbow. Then—and this is the essential technique in this sequence—the defender pulls in with the right hand and pushes out with the left forearm (fig. 9.26–27). (In the first sequence, the reverse of this is shown; that is, the left hand pulls in while the right forearm pushes out against the attacker's elbow.) The effect of this pressure on the attacker's elbow moves the opponent, bringing him or her forward and down. As the defender steps forward into horse stance, facing the original front of the kata, the left arm is brought over and around the opponent's neck (fig. 9.28).

This is often described as something akin to carrying a football and often mistakenly interpreted as catching an opponent's kicking foot. The problem with that interpretation—other than the fact that it's unrealistic—is that it fails to take into account the techniques that lead into it and, indeed, the techniques that follow it. It's important when analyzing kata to see the combinations, to be able to identify the beginnings and the endings.

FIGURE 9.26.

FIGURE 9.27.

FIGURES 9.26–28. Continuing the sequence, the opponent is brought forward and down with the forearm pressing on the elbow. Then, stepping into horse stance, the front hand grabs the head while the rear hand comes over and around the neck.

FIGURE 9.29. In this position, which suggests Da Vinci's *Vitruvian Man*, the hands have been pulled apart, one holding the opponent's chin as the other held the top of the head.

FIGURE 9.30. In the arms-up position, the opponent's body has been turned around.

FIGURE 9.31. The hands are brought down, throwing the opponent over the hip and then attacking in a deep horse stance.

In this next technique, the final technique of this sequence, the left, lower hand grabs the attacker's chin, while the right, upper hand grabs the head. Then both hands are pulled apart forcefully, twisting the attacker's head and, at the same time, causing the attacker's body to turn in the direction of the head twist (fig. 9.29).

In this position, with the attacker's body in back of the defender and the attacker's head in front, the defender's arm along the opponent's throat (fig. 9.30), the defender then drops into a low horse stance, bringing both arms down in front, throwing the opponent over the left hip, and attacking with the right palm (fig. 9.31). This low attack may be a palm strike or, crossing the hands, a neck break.

Fourth Sequence

The fourth sequence begins with an upper-level block (fig. 9.32). Like the first sequence, the attack is from the front. But unlike the other three sequences of the kata, this sequence is only shown on one side— the rising left arm block against a left arm attack. In some schools, the hands are rotated an extra time in the upper position or brought down and back up again to show the hand position if one were to do the other side, but there is nothing else shown of the left-side position, like a left-foot-forward front stance stepping to the northwest angle, for example.

The defender's left arm is brought up vertically, with the elbow down, to intercept the opponent's attack (fig. 9.33). This technique is very similar to the third sequence of the kata and to the upper-level blocking technique we see in Saifa. Additionally, one could execute this technique from the previous horse stance—that is, without committing oneself to a step to either side of the attacker—or one could use the stepping shown in kata to move to the side, avoiding the attack, as the arm is brought up.

In any case, the left arm is blocking, with both hands rotating as the defender turns 180 degrees counterclockwise, bringing both feet together, to face the south. As the defender pivots, the left hand grabs the attacker's wrist on the outside and the right hand rotates underneath to grab the attacker's wrist on the inside. Then, as the defender drops into a squatting position, the attacker is thrown (fig. 9.34).

FIGURE 9.32. Stepping forward on an angle to block a head attack

FIGURE 9.33. Both blocking hands are to the outside of the attack.

FIGURE 9.34. Position after the throw

Once the opponent is thrown, the defender steps in to attack the head (fig. 9.37). This technique is shown on both the left and right sides, with a step into a left-foot-forward front stance and a right-foot-forward front stance. It is unlikely (though certainly possible) that both of these techniques are meant to be applied to the same opponent, particularly in addition to the final *mawashi* or head twist. It is far more likely that the stepping techniques are shown twice because, regardless of which throw the defender executes, against the opponent's right arm or left arm, where and how the opponent falls is somewhat unpredictable. So again, we have a somewhat unique structure for a kata sequence, though one that is fairly clear.

Most schools will interpret each of these last two front stance techniques, executed to the rear angles of the kata, as either a block against an opponent's front kick with the front hand and a grab of the opponent's foot with the other hand (fig. 9.35), or, alternatively, as a grab of the opponent's foot and an attack to the side of the opponent's knee (fig. 9.36). However, the problem is that once again the entire sequence is not taken into account—that is, it ignores the throw, which in itself is not a finishing technique.

FIGURE 9.35. Common interpretation of this technique

FIGURE 9.36. Another common interpretation of this technique

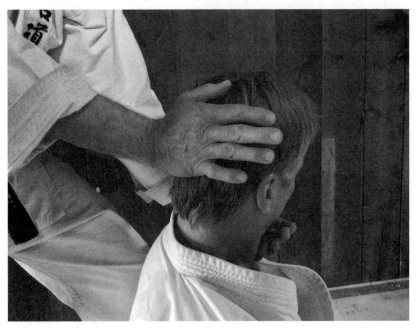

FIGURE 9.37. The technique that would occur after throwing the opponent

Of course there would be a farewell party before we left, with speeches and a lot of food. It was a tradition. We spent the last week shopping for little presents—we had made a lot of friends in Okinawa. Kimo sensei had to leave the island early to fly back to the States, so he asked me to speak for him at the farewell dinner. I spent the next few afternoons with Reiko in the coffee shop, translating the speech into phoneticized Japanese that I could read, not knowing all of the words but learning to pronounce them well enough to be understood.

Then one night, walking home after dinner, we spotted Matayoshi sensei coming toward us dressed in a *yukata*, an informal summer kimono. He was carrying a *sanshin* (Okinawan *shamisen*) that he had made, with a rich black lacquer body and snake skin covering the sound box. He handed me the *shamisen* and told us he'd meet us at our apartment in a few minutes. When he came up, we sat down on the tatami mats as Sensei explained all about the *shamisen*. Then he told me to keep it and practice. When I protested, as politely as I could, that I could never afford such a beautiful instrument, he just laughed, telling me to check around and then give him a price. He added that he had loosened the snake skin so that hopefully it wouldn't split when I took it back to America—snake skins being highly sensitive to changes in heat and humidity.

I realized then that there was no way I could repay Matayoshi sensei for everything he had done for us that summer. It was a sad farewell, especially since, thinking back on it now, Matayoshi sensei has since passed on, and my fellow student, who shared many of these memories of that summer with me, died all too young. I did see Matayoshi sensei again when I returned to Okinawa the following year, and then again when he stayed with us in Massachusetts for a short time the year Kimo sensei took him on a historic tour

FIGURE 9.38. The *shamisen* Matayoshi gave the author. Even with the precautions, the skin still split.

of the United States. He laughed with us, and joked, and played with my children, pushing my daughter around the driveway on her tricycle.

We had a seminar at the University of Massachusetts Amherst that year, and Matayoshi sensei taught *kobudo*. Students came from all over. During a break, one of the students wanted to show Sensei his White Crane kata—Kakuho from Matayoshi's Kingai-ryu. Partway through the form, Matayoshi turned, rolled his eyes, and whispered, "Video." When the student finished, Sensei asked, "Who teach?" That part wasn't clear.

Matayoshi sensei would often ask that question. Sometimes he was just curious how things had changed, as if there was a sort of etymology of kata movements. Sometimes he would say, "Oh, yeah, yeah, old way. OK." But at other times, there seemed to be a challenge to the question, as if you were being cross-examined after being caught with your hand in the cookie jar. Matayoshi sensei never performed the kata the same way in public, always wary of what he called "stealy boys" who might videotape techniques in order to teach themselves kata. And yet he was still kind enough, on this occasion, to offer the student a few corrections.

FIGURE 9.39. Matayoshi with the author's daughter Emily

Kata did change sometimes, I realized. Once in Matayoshi's dojo, when he was calling us through Suparinpei, I remember him saying, toward the end of the kata, *"Hidari yon ju go"* (to the left 45). When we went straight back into horse stance, because we had been doing the kata the way it was done then in the Shodokan-Higa dojo, instead of at an angle, Sensei looked at us quizzically for just a moment and then said, "Yeah, OK."

The changes to different kata had bothered me that summer in Okinawa. Kururunfa, which we had always begun to the left, now started to the right. And when it finished, with the two long front stances, it now went first to the left and then to the right, and then finished in a right-foot-forward cat stance. I was confused. Why did different schools—founded by teachers who had all trained under Miyagi Chojun sensei—do kata differently? But when I finally asked Gibo sensei, he just looked at me and said, "Why not?"

FIGURE 9.40. The author and his wife, Martha, at Matayoshi sensei's house for dinner

10

壱百零八手

SUPARINPEI

FIGURE 10.1. A variation of the final technique of the kata

THE LAST KATA IN THE CANON of Goju-ryu classical subjects is gener-ally considered to be Suparinpei, sometimes referred to as Pechurin. It is thought to be the most advanced of the Kaishu kata, though why that is the case is difficult to say. While it is the longest of these kata, it is also the kata with the most redundancy of technique. Techniques in Suparinpei sometimes occur singly, sometimes in pairs, sometimes in groups of three or four techniques. It is also one of only two kata in the classical canon where the *embusen* (pattern of movement) shows techniques done in each of the eight compass directions, recalling the admonition of the "Hakku Kempo" that "the eyes see in four directions" and "the ears hear in eight directions." So there are many things about the structure of Suparinpei that are unique, not to be found in the other classical subjects.

The kanji that is usually used for Suparinpei, 壱百零八, is generally translated as "108." More than likely, as seems to be the case with the other kata that reference numbers, this is not a reference to the number of techniques in the kata but rather to Buddhist numerological symbol-ism—the 108 here a reference to the belief that humanity is plagued with 108 mortal passions. Whether Buddhism had a significant influence on the development of karate or not, this is actually a quite well-founded tra-dition in both Chinese and Japanese culture. The last day of the year, one can hear the temple bells ringing 108 times all over Japan and Okinawa. And in light of Sanchin, thought to represent three metaphorical battles, it is not surprising that the practice of a kata might take on this sort of significance. After all, this is a culture where the tea ceremony and flower arranging are practiced as spiritual endeavors.

There have been other explanations, of course. Some have suggested that the number 108 may have been an oblique reference to the Outlaws of the Marsh, the 108 bandit-heroes depicted in the Chinese classic *Shui Hu Zhuan* (retold in English by Pearl S. Buck in her book *All Men Are Brothers*). Set in the ancient Song Dynasty, the story follows the exploits of a group of renegade warriors who rob from the rich to give to the poor, trying to right the wrongs they see around them. Others have suggested that the origin of the kata and its techniques may be traced to Yue Fei, a Chinese general who taught 108 empty-hand fighting techniques that came to be called Yue Shi San Shou (Yue Fei's Fighting Techniques), eventually becoming the basis of Eagle Claw kung fu. And at least one researcher has suggested that the number 108 may be a reference to ancient Chinese star charts, that the number should be understood as a reference to "the heavens"—that is, the kata, just as the heavens, is all-encompassing, that it is "all about the techniques and principles taught in this or that Quan Fa school."[1] The problem here, however, is that Suparinpei, while it does reference many of the techniques of Sanseiru and Seisan, does not encompass the entire system or even a significant percentage of the techniques that we find in the rest of the classical subjects, unless, of course, as some have suggested, Saifa, Seiunchin, Shisochin, Seipai, and Kururunfa were later additions. In any case, none of these theories about the origin of the kata name tells us much about the techniques themselves.

In addition, legend has it that there may have been as many as three separate Suparinpei kata—a *jodan* level, *chudan* level, and *gedan* level version—with only one version of the kata having been preserved. There is, however, no solid proof of this either, and speculation along these lines only feeds into the mystique of the kata—that is, if there were three distinct versions, then perhaps only fragments of each were somehow passed on, hence the fragmented nature of the structure.

Indeed, it is the structure of Suparinpei that raises so many questions for Goju-ryu practitioners. Unlike the other classical kata composed in large part of sequences that illustrate specific *bunkai,* Suparinpei is for the most part a collection of separate entry, controlling, and finishing techniques, with only three complete *bunkai* sequences. In this sense, Suparinpei most resembles Seisan with its three sets of three entry techniques at the beginning of the kata. But even Seisan is mainly composed of *bunkai* sequences that illustrate its themes, and the entry techniques are all situated at the beginning of the kata.

Suparinpei, on the other hand, is a mix of techniques, not just entry techniques, and put together in such a way as to suggest that any entry technique or any controlling technique might be put together with any of the finishing techniques. It's exactly the way one might put together a kata if one's primary focus was to protect the style's secrets, to hide them, as it were, from prying eyes. This open-ended structure, sort of like a random collection of basics stuck together in kata form, is reminiscent of some kung fu forms, where only individual techniques are practiced, leaving it up to the instructor to provide one with context and application. Most of the techniques of Suparinpei could, in fact, be executed in a straight line, as some kung fu forms are; but the kata pattern, emphasizing both the cardinal and ordinal compass points, is a reminder to students of the principle of off-line movement.

So, given the cryptic nature of its structure and the fact that there are few resemblances here to the other classical kata, how does one begin a study of Suparinpei? What is essential to an understanding of the kata when the kata itself seems to be so atypical? How did a kata that seems so atypical come to be included in a collection where all of the other kata share so many similarities? Was the kata left unfinished, as one of my students suggests? Or does it merely show "seed" techniques, a distillation of everything we see in the other classical subjects, as another student suggests?

I'm reminded of something Jimmy Bigelow says in Richard Flanagan's *The Narrow Road to the Deep North*. "The bigger the mystery, the more it means," he says, though I think more accurately, especially in this case, it might read, "The bigger the mystery, the more we *think* it means." Earlier in the same novel, there is a discussion about *go,* the Chinese board game, and how one can become adept at this difficult game. Sato, one of the characters, responds, "There is a pattern and structure to all things. Only we can't see it. Our job is to discover that pattern and structure and work within it, as part of it." That, I believe, is what we have to do with all of the kata, but it is essential to an understanding of Suparinpei.

The beginning:

Suparinpei kata—one of the kata that starts from the double-arm *kamae* position (fig. 10.2)—begins with three steps in basic stance and three slow punches, reminiscent of Sanseiru kata. Like Shisochin, Seisan, and Sanseiru, these techniques illustrate responses to a clinch or two-arm grappling starting posture. They should be seen not so much as punches as a sort of pushing and pulling for advantage, or as an opportunity to study the pushing and pulling of the opponent in an attempt to unbalance or gain an advantage (fig. 10.3).

When using these techniques in practicing with a partner, the idea is to train one's sensitivity or listening skills. This is the reason, I believe, some of them are done slowly. In theory, all of the entry techniques in this kata begin from this position. When we study this with a partner, we can use any of the positions that this posture represents—both arms inside our partner's arms, both arms on the outside, one inside and one outside, or one pushing and the other coming up to block. Each position should be studied as a precursor to the entry and controlling techniques that follow in the kata.

The next technique, occurring only once in the kata, is another release technique. Both hands are brought inside the opponent's arms (figs. 10.4 and 10.6) and then thrust straight out to either side (figs. 10.5 and 10.7), but one should note that the collapsing or inward motion of the arms is just as important in the execution of this technique as the outward motion. And it may be executed from the *kamae* or clinch position if the defender's arms are on the outside or the inside of the attacker's arms. Because of the structure of the kata, however, the follow-up to this initial movement—what would ordinarily be the controlling and finishing techniques—is not shown. In fact, each of these techniques at the beginning of Suparinpei—the three slow punches that precede this and the series of

FIGURE 10.2. Suparinpei is another of the kata that begins in the double-arm *kamae* posture.

mawashi techniques that follow—show initial or entry techniques without being clearly connected to a complete *bunkai* sequence in the same way that we would find it in the other classical subjects.

FIGURE 10.3. Using the slow punch to disrupt the opponent's balance and escape the clinch

FIGURES 10.4–5. The spreading arms technique in kata

FIGURES 10.6–7. Another of the fundamental techniques used against the opponent's clinch

The next technique:

The four sets of *mawashi uke* techniques, each paired, are done in opposite directions (or opposite rotation of the arms) with a forward step in basic stance accompanying each and executed to the four cardinal compass points. They all begin with the same side in a left-foot-forward basic stance, with the same initial turning block in a counterclockwise direction, and each finishing with a right hand grab and left palm-up *nukite* reminiscent of the first sequence in Seiunchin kata. However, unlike the *mawashi* techniques that occur in the other classical kata, the *mawashi* techniques here, at the beginning of Suparinpei, are done in basic stance moving forward. This is very important. The stance itself implies the difference in application. These *mawashi* techniques are used as "blocking" techniques—that is, they function as initial entry and controlling techniques, as opposed to finishing techniques, which is what we see elsewhere in the classical subjects.

FIGURE 10.8.

FIGURE 10.9.

FIGURES 10.8–10. The *mawashi* technique used against the opponent's clinch

MAWASHI UKE

There has been a lot written about the mawashi uke. *Some of it has been couched in questions about the possible origins of Goju-ryu kata—a subject that opens up endless bandying about of theory based on little more than observation, interpretation, or personal bias. Some of this, of course, is prompted by individuals promoting their own lineage or traditions with little actual evidence to go on other than the perceived similarity of appearances.*

And this is what has always interested me in discussions of this sort— they are all based on appearances, and appearances, as we all know, can be deceiving. For example: Some would suggest that Saifa kata and Seisan kata must have similar origins because they both end in cat stance with a kind of mawashi uke. Others, however, would suggest that Saifa was a kata that came not from Higashionna sensei but from Miyagi sensei, because Kyoda sensei didn't teach Saifa. Some suggest that the Okinawan katas came originally from China because we can find similar postures—cat stance with what looks like the ending hand positions of mawashi uke or tora guchi—in various Chinese systems. What really needs to be compared, however, are the applications, or the bunkai, if you will, of the various postures.

The mawashi uke is actually not as ubiquitous as it would seem, outside Goju-ryu training kata like Geki-sai Dai Ichi, Geki-sai Dai Ni, Gekiha, or some of the other training subjects practiced in various Goju-ryu schools. There is, in fact, no mawashi uke in Seiunchin or Shisochin or Sanseiru, though there are open-hand techniques and we see circular movements. A kind of mawashi uke occurs at the end of Saifa, but it's not necessarily the same as the one we find at the end of Sanchin kata. And the same may be said of the mawashi uke in the middle of Kururunfa or the end technique of Seipai.

My point is that it's difficult, if not misleading, only to compare appearances, when any perceived similarity in appearance is clearly secondary to how a technique is meant to be applied (not how it could be applied). It's a martial art, after all, not a dance performance. A number of years ago, there was an article published—and it received widespread notice and still does to this day—that attempted to classify the Goju-ryu classical kata according to their appearances.[2] Did they end in cat stance or horse stance? Were they symmetrical or asymmetrical? But if we are going to study the relationships between the different kata of Goju-ryu, we should be studying the bunkai of the techniques in kata, not their outward appearances. The mawashi at the end of Saifa is meant to capture and twist the head of the opponent—to break the neck or traumatize the spinal cord, if you will. The ending mawashi-like technique of Seipai is intended to do the same thing, and yet it looks very different. So is the mawashi in the middle of Kururunfa. And the one at the end of Seisan. They are all used for the same purpose, but they are situation-specific, so they look a little different.

My suggestion: put kata in its place. It's a useful method to remember the form of technique and perhaps to study the thematic nature of certain movements or techniques. But put the emphasis back on bunkai, on the study of application. Comparing techniques based solely on appearance is problematic to say the least. Suparinpei is a case in point, because both types of mawashi techniques appear in this kata—one used as an entry and controlling technique and one used as a finishing technique.

The *mawashi* "blocks" are once again a release technique against the opponent's arms in the clinch position. Each pair of *mawashi* techniques—though they are not meant to be used together—shows the release technique being used to fold the opponent's arms and move to the outside. The clinch or two-handed grab position that this series illustrates begins with the defender's arms on the outside of the attacker's arms. The first of these *mawashi* techniques begins with the defender's right arm coming up while pushing in and the defender's left arm going down while pushing in (fig. 10.8). It is important that both arms are pushing in against the two arms of the attacker. In this first *mawashi* technique, the defender's left arm then comes underneath the attacker's left arm so that the defender is now on the outside of the attacker. Stepping forward, this technique is then shown on the other side, working against the opposite side of the opponent. And finally, the *mawashi* technique continues with the right hand being brought up to grab the attacker's head (fig. 10.9) while the left *"nukite"* comes in to attack the throat and control the chin, just as it does in Seiunchin kata (fig. 10.10). This is the controlling technique in this sequence, and it is only shown on one side (as a continuation of the first *mawashi uke*). Again, this is an incomplete sequence since it doesn't show the finishing technique; however, the kata does show a number of finishing techniques that might be employed here, from the *mawashi* in cat stance that follows this series, to the "double punch" series that is shown a bit later in the kata, to the finishing technique of the first complete sequence (fig. 10.26).

The next technique:

The next two techniques—the first repeated three times, and the second repeated four times—are finishing techniques. The first of these is another *mawashi* technique, but this time done in cat stance (fig. 10.11). Again, the stance implies the difference in application. This *mawashi* is employed as a finishing technique using the knee kick that the stance implies. This is the same *mawashi* finishing technique that we find in the other classical subjects. There is a strong suggestion here that the two different *mawashi* techniques we find in Suparinpei were probably done differently at one time as well—that without a proper understanding of their functions, their movements were homogenized.

In any case, the first of these finishing techniques is placed here in the kata because it could be attached to the end of the paired *mawashi* blocking or release techniques. It could, of course, also serve as a finishing technique at the end of many other sequences, as we see in the other classical subjects.

FIGURE 10.11. The *mawashi uke* in cat stance

FIGURES 10.12–13. The "double punch," used much the same way as it is in Sanseiru kata, is one of the controlling/finishing techniques that comes off the initial *mawashi uke*.

The second finishing technique here, following the three *mawashi* techniques and repeated four times, is the double punch technique done to the four cardinal compass points (figs. 10.12–13). This is the same double-punching technique we see at the end of Sanseiru, and it is used the same way, as a head-twisting neck break. Again, it too may be attached to the end of the double *mawashi* opening techniques by simply closing the open palm-up *nukite* around the opponent's chin, pulling down with the right hand, and thrusting out and overtop with the left hand that is closed around the opponent's chin (fig. 10.14).

FIGURE 10.14. Close-up of both hands on the head before reversing the hands to twist the head, what is often referred to as a parry and punch.

The next technique:

The next technique in this beginning section of Suparinpei kata has a similar function to the preceding techniques—that is, it is a controlling technique attached to the *mawashi* release techniques. So in that sense, it is neither an entry technique nor a finishing technique. It is done dropping into horse stance (fig. 10.15), and advancing along an angle or the ordinal compass points. These angular advancing steps in horse stance are reminiscent of Sei-unchin kata, and, indeed, the technique itself should remind one of the front corner techniques in Seiunchin or the rear corner techniques in Seipai kata.

FIGURE 10.15. The horse stance blocking techniques are used after the mawashi uke.

FIGURE 10.16.   FIGURE 10.17.

FIGURE 10.18.

FIGURE 10.19.

FIGURES 10.16–20. Using the horse stance corner techniques against an attacker

We can see an example of how this technique is used with the *mawashi* release technique. From the clinch position or the opponent's grab, using the first part of the *mawashi* technique, the defender's right arm pushes in against the attacker's left arm (fig. 10.16). Then, moving to the outside and dropping into horse stance, the defender's left arm comes under and across to the outside of the attacker's left arm, palm up (fig. 10.17). This is the position we see in kata. It's important to remember that none of these positions that we see in still photographs, or held for any length of time in the performance of kata, are static. There should be no gaps; fluid, continuous movement in the execution of any sequence of moves against an opponent should be the rule.

Once the left arm is brought up to block, the palm immediately turns to guard against the attacker's elbow (fig. 10.18) and, advancing along the diagonal, the right hand attacks the opponent's head (fig. 10.19), grabbing and bringing it down into the right knee of the horse stance (fig. 10.20). What would seem to be missing here is the finishing technique that we see in Seiunchin—the step back into a left-foot-forward horse stance with a left downward forearm strike to the back of the neck. However, if we consider the angles of attack in reference to the execution of this technique, our view of this technique may be slightly different. Instead of turning and dropping into horse stance to face an attacker from the southeast corner, as is shown in the first of these techniques—what would effectively suggest moving away from the attacker for the initial block—we might imagine that we are in a clinch position facing west. In this position, dropping into horse stance brings us over the attacker's left shoulder, slightly to his rear angle. In this position, the left hand is close enough to attack and control the opponent's chin, while the defender's right hand comes forward to grab the hair (queue, in ancient times) or control the head. Then, stepping through into a right-foot-forward horse stance, the countering force of the right and left hands twists the opponent's head. This way of looking at the technique, without altering the kata movement, brings it more thematically in line with the rest of the kata. However, this may in fact be looking for a complete *bunkai* sequence where none is actually intended. If we alter the movements of kata, however small those alterations may be, the effort doesn't seem worth the sacrifice. What seems more likely is that this technique, like many of the other techniques in Suparinpei, illustrates just that—a technique that is only part of an incomplete sequence.

First Sequence

The first two complete sequences of Suparinpei kata are very similar. This first sequence shows two open-hand blocks, a kick, and an elbow attack to the head followed by a neck break. This is the first combination in Suparinpei that shows an entry, controlling or bridging techniques, and a finishing technique. Beginning from the previous technique, the sequence starts with the left foot stepping forward and the left arm moving in a clockwise, semicircular fashion with the palm or forearm pressing down and finishing in the *gedan* position. Then the right foot steps forward into basic stance with the right arm moving up in a clockwise semicircular fashion with the palm facing forward (figs. 10.21–22). The opening two-hand blocking motion we see here is reminiscent of the sun and moon block found in the Shodokan version of Seisan kata. It is unusual in the Goju-ryu classical subjects to see an initial blocking technique stepping forward. However, if we imagine starting from a clinch position, the blocking and unbalancing nature of these moves makes more sense.

Following the initial entry techniques, the left foot steps forward again and the left arm is brought up with the left hand over the opponent's shoulder (fig. 10.23). In the Shodokan-Higa version of Suparinpei, this technique will look very much like the front hand of the four-direction technique in Shisochin kata. Other versions of the kata will simply add an additional step forward in basic stance and a left open-hand block. In either case, from here the defender kicks with the right foot as the left hand brings the attacker's head in for a right horizontal elbow attack (fig. 10.24). The defender's right arm then unfolds, bringing it behind the opponent's head (fig. 10.25). Then, grabbing the back of the head or topknot, the left hand is brought around to the opponent's chin (fig. 10.26). The final move, shown only in this first sequence, shows the defender pushing out with the left hand as the right hand pulls in, twisting the opponent's head and breaking the neck.

FIGURES 10.21–22. The first position of the first full sequence, shown from the kata and against an opponent

FIGURE 10.23. The first full sequence continues with this technique from Shisochin, bringing the left arm up alongside the opponent's head.

FIGURE 10.24.

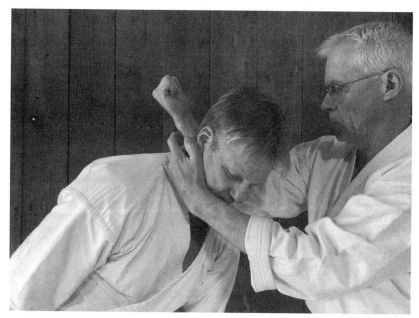

FIGURE 10.25.

FIGURES 10.24–26. After the kick, there is a horizontal elbow attack to the head followed by a neck break.

It should be noted that this is a very fast technique and of course very dangerous to practice. In fact, all of the finishing techniques found in the classical subjects should be approached with extreme caution when working with a partner. It should also be noted that the beginning position of this technique—when the defender's arm unfolds, bringing it behind the opponent's head—is similar to the raised arm position in the fourth sequence of Seiunchin kata. In that sequence, the arm is brought down in what looks like a lower-level attack, bringing the head with it in order to step back and attack the head with the other forearm. What is particularly noteworthy is that any time one finds oneself in this position relative to the opponent, with the forearm along the outside of the neck and able to use the other hand, either of these *bunkai* "solutions" should be readily available.

The next technique:

After this first sequence, and before the second sequence, the kata again seems to show a short series of entry and controlling techniques. The first of these occurs on the turn around and is reminiscent of the same series of techniques in Seisan kata. In Seisan, however, this series of entry and controlling techniques is done twice (though some schools will practice this four times, two for each side) because the controlling techniques go together. In Suparinpei, they are shown three times and not connected to finishing techniques, as they are in Seisan. This emphasizes the fundamental or basic nature of these techniques. In other words, the kata leaves it open as to which finishing techniques one might use after this series. The functional part of the series consists of the first two techniques, the turning right arm block and left palm strike (fig. 10.27) followed by a step into a right-foot-forward basic stance with the left arm coming down along the outside of the attacker's left arm and the defender's right coming up to grab the head (fig. 10.28). This is a "changing gate" technique. The first technique blocks on the outside and then, because of its circular nature, moves to the inside with the attack. The second technique moves to the outside, turning the attacker, to position the defender to the back side of the opponent.

FIGURES 10.27–28. These two fundamental entry techniques are used much the same as they are in Seisan kata.

The next technique:

The next technique is an open left hand block followed by a right crescent kick (figs. 10.29–30). Again, this technique, done with a complete 360-degree turn, doesn't seem to be part of any sequence. Because of that, it's almost impossible to determine how it was meant to be used. The same extended arm block and crescent kick can be found in Shorin-ryu kata, but it doesn't occur anywhere else in the classical kata of Goju-ryu.

It is often shown as a sweeping technique to unbalance or take the opponent down (figs. 10.31–32). Sometimes it is used defensively against an opponent's kick or to grab the opponent's arm and break the elbow. A few have even shown the crescent kick used to come over the top of the opponent's arm, trapping the arm between the legs, and then pulling up on the arm. This seems a bit of a stretch to me, and not necessarily a position I would like to find myself in if I were the defender. The most likely use of the crescent kick, and the most realistic, would seem to be as a defensive technique against an opponent's kick or as a sweep to momentarily unbalance the opponent. In either case, however, it is difficult to imagine why one would need to turn completely around when dealing with an opponent.

FIGURE 10.29.

FIGURES 10.29–30. The block and crescent kick

FIGURES 10.31–32. Using the crescent kick

As a defensive technique or as a sweep against the opponent's front leg, especially from a clinch, the hand and foot techniques might very easily follow the initial *mawashi uke* entry technique, tying together this technique and the sequence that follows.

Next Sequence

The next complete sequence is very similar to the first sequence but with a jumping kick. The neck twist is not usually shown. This series of techniques—the two open-hand blocks, the jumping front kick, and the elbow attack—could easily be viewed as a complete sequence on its own. However, it might also be seen as a continuation of the pervious block and crescent kick, especially if we begin from the clinch and use the *mawashi* technique as a release. In this scenario, after the block, grab, and crescent kick, the defender's right arm comes down onto the attacker's left arm, and the defender's left arm comes up alongside the attacker's head or grabs the shoulder. Then the defender jumps, kicking with the right knee or foot and continuing with the horizontal elbow attack to the opponent's head, the same as in the first sequence.

Last Sequence

The last sequence borrows much from both Seisan kata and Sanseiru kata. It begins on the turn around into basic stance, with a right counterclockwise circular block and a left open-hand attack to the face. This is a simultaneous block and attack, typical of Goju-ryu classical kata and seen three times in Seisan kata.

The defender then shifts forward into a left-foot-forward horse stance—advancing on and unbalancing the opponent—the arms making two circular blocking motions, as in the second sequence of Seisan kata. This is the controlling or bridging technique. In Seisan kata, as the defender shifts forward, the left arm drops down along the attacker's left arm, safeguarding against the attacker's elbow, as the right hand comes up to attack the head and grab the hair or topknot. Seisan shows one

FIGURE 10.33. This kata position is reminiscent of Seisan, but what follows it is reminiscent of Sanseiru.

variation of the technique that we see here. Since the hands are kept open in Suparinpei, however, the other variation we see in Seisan may be more appropriate here. That is, after the initial block and counterattack, the defender maintains contact with the attacker's left arm, bringing it up and over, as it is transferred to the defender's left arm, while the defender drops under it, shifting forward into horse stance. At this point, the right hand comes forward in what looks like a spear hand thrust and the left hand is brought back, with the left palm resting on the right upper arm or shoulder joint (fig. 10.33). This technique is reminiscent of the straight "punch" at the end of Seisan kata, except that in Suparinpei the hands are open during this entire sequence. The closed hands of Seisan kata show one variation of this technique—that is, the grabbing and control of the hair and the chin in order to twist the head. In Suparinpei, all that is necessary is that the right arm is thrust out past the opponent's head and the left hand is used to bring the head in toward the shoulder (fig. 10.34).

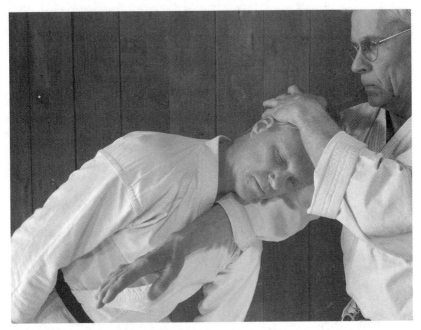

FIGURE 10.34. Bringing the head in

FIGURE 10.35. This final position is reminiscent of Sanseiru, but there are also differences.

In the last move of the kata (fig. 10.35)—the step and turn to the original front—the left hand comes under the opponent's chin, palm up, as the right arm folds in. Then stepping around to face the front, the left hand pulls the opponent's chin up while the right hand pushes down on the top of the head, twisting the head and breaking the neck. In the performance of this kata in most schools, the right arm is drawn inside and over the left as it circles in before it is brought up in the final or ending position. The implication here is that the opponent's chin is in the left hand, just as it is in the final technique of Sanseiru kata. And, in fact, the final technique in each kata could be done the same.

However, there is an old saying in Goju-ryu schools, passed on through oral tradition, that there is a difference between the ending techniques of Sanseiru and Suparinpei, even though the final position may look the same. In one kata, it is said, the technique goes down, and in the other, it goes up. One can certainly appreciate the simplicity of this instruction in practice. However, separated by long years or even generations of students who

FIGURE 10.36. Differing from Sanseiru, the right hand comes under to grab the chin.

may only have preserved this admonition in the practice of their kata, not having any experience of its application, we can only guess at what it may have meant. My guess is that it refers to a variation of how one might execute this final technique in Suparinpei—that is, in turning to the front, the right hand, instead of the left, may take the opponent's chin and pull up, with the left hand pushing down on the top of the head (fig. 10.36). The same thing is accomplished—twisting the head and breaking the neck—but in a manner that differentiates Suparinpei kata from Sanseiru kata.

Most of the restaurants were closed for New Year's, so Matayoshi sensei took pity on us and invited us up to the house for dinner. This was the second year we came to take advantage of Matayoshi's hospitality, and I felt a little like an interloper. There were so many important teachers who came to pay their respects to Sensei that evening. In between visitors, Sensei pulled out a scroll of his family tree, tracing his family back over four hundred years. He was very proud that the tradition of *kobudo* in

FIGURE 10.37. New Year's at Matayoshi's house

his family went back generations. I'm not sure they all practiced *kobudo*, but the martial tradition in his family did go quite far back. And the point was, as he said, that once upon a time there were many different martial traditions, but over time they got pared down. The bad ones died off, because in the old days you had to use your martial arts to survive. If *you* didn't survive the battle or the confrontation, neither did your martial art. Those who survived passed their systems on to others. We don't generally use our martial arts in battles or confrontations of the sort that might have been more commonplace in ancient times. Consequently, there isn't the same sort of natural selection at work nowadays. Some things certainly die out on their own—extinction may be more the rule than preservation, as paleoanthropologist Richard Leakey says—but the odds and ends of rubble and detritus seem the order of the day in this age of information. Anyone can find anything on the internet, and it's all terribly democratic—anyone can become an expert.

I once learned a *bo* kata from a friend who trained in a traditional karate dojo. As a rule, they didn't do very much *kobudo*—after all, *kobudo* is really a separate tradition—but their teacher had taught them this one *bo* kata. I spent about thirty minutes following my friend through the moves of the kata before I realized that it was Sakugawa no kon, a kata I already knew. What had momentarily confused me was the fact that they had been taught the mirror-image of the kata; everything was backward. Not that there's anything wrong with doing a kata backward, but I suspect that the teacher had taught himself from watching a video.

The problem is that some things can't be taught through videos or books. There are some things I have trouble teaching students *in the dojo.* You have to see it and realize what you're seeing in order to practice it. You can teach the moves, but not the movement. I'm reminded of some of the principles talked about in the Chinese classics and that can be found in Douglas Wile's *T'ai-Chi Touchstones: Yang Family Secret Transmissions.* Here are a few: "All the joints of the body should be connected without permitting the slightest break." "Power issues from the back." "At all times bear in mind and consciously remember that as soon as one part of the body moves, the whole body moves." "Do not allow gaps."

It's all so poetic and cryptic because it's difficult to teach ... and just as difficult to talk about. It's almost as if the phrases are only reminders, only useful if you already understand what they mean.

I got a phone call from Kimo Wall sensei one morning. It was about a year after I last saw Matayoshi sensei, who had stayed with me for a week the summer Kimo sensei took him on a driving tour of the States. He would die the following year. I knew that Kimo sensei had decided to visit Okinawa again that year and maybe to go on to mainland China, stopping in Fujian Province, as so many great masters before him had, to visit the roots of Okinawan karate. We knew the stories, of course, that all of the great masters had left China during the Cultural Revolution, but the stories did little to dampen the desire to see the places for oneself or that perhaps there was the slightest chance that there was something that others had missed.

Kimo sensei had stopped off in Taiwan to visit friends, students he had taught in the States but who were now working in Taiwan. One day, out for a walk, they stopped in a local bookstore to look at the martial arts books. Kimo sensei noticed a book on Eating (Feeding) Crane kung fu and began leafing through it, looking at the pictures. It reminded him of Goju-ryu technique. The book was by a Master Liu, and they noticed from the book jacket that he lived in a village not far from where they were.

After returning home, they made a few phone calls and were told they were welcome to stop by the family residence. When they arrived, however, they learned that Master Liu had died. But in a conversation with Master Liu's brother, they found out that there had been contact between Master Liu and Okinawa. Uncle Liu brought out a photograph that showed Master Liu with Higa Seikichi and Takamine Chotoku, leaders in the Shodokan school of Okinawan Goju-ryu, and teachers whom Kimo sensei was personally close to.

Later that day, Kimo sensei met Sifu Liu Chang-I, the lineage heir to the Feeding Crane system and son of the Master Liu who had written the book Kimo sensei had seen in the bookstore. They demonstrated kata for each other, talked, laughed, and quickly became close friends. And seeing Sifu Liu do kata, Kimo sensei heard what he would later call "thunder" emanating from Liu's body. It was a power within the body that could be unleashed at very short range. Sifu called it short power or "inchy power."

It was a kind of *fa jing* developed by a special set of exercises that Liu referred to simply as *kung li*. When Kimo sensei heard it—the sound that emanated from Sifu Liu's body when he made any of these short, powerful movements so characteristic of the Feeding Crane system—he was dumbstruck. He had heard the stories about Miyagi Chojun sensei having "thunder" in his body since he was a small boy first learning karate in Hawaii. All of the elders had said that when Miyagi sensei did kata, "He had thunder in his body. You could hear it." And now he had, once again, found it. It wasn't just a legend.

FIGURE 10.38. Kimo Wall sensei (left) and Sifu Liu Chang-I in front of the author's barn dojo

I heard the story over the phone that morning when Kimo sensei called me from Taiwan. He was excited. He had found something that he believed had been a part of Okinawan karate in the past but had somehow been lost over the years, and he wanted to bring it back to the States, along with Sifu Liu. It wasn't a new kata or a collection of techniques but a way of moving. You can learn techniques and kata from books and videos, but it's much harder to learn how to move. It's something quite profound. I suppose that's the irony of trying to write a book about any martial tradition, not just Goju-ryu; it's really hard to put it into words, the important stuff. About the best you can do, I guess, like someone trying to explain Zen Buddhism, is to point at the moon.

AFTERWORD

Studying karate nowadays is like walking in the dark without a lantern.

—MIYAGI CHOJUN SENSEI

CERTAINLY THERE IS MORE to karate than kata and *bunkai,* something more than learning how to defend yourself. It's also something a bit more intangible and harder to put into words. Perhaps this is what Miyagi sensei was referring to when he said that the "physical and mental unity" that one gets from training karate "develops an indomitable spirit." Miyagi himself seemed to suggest this spiritual side to training the martial arts in his "Karate-Do Gaisetsu: An Outline of Karate-Do." He says here that karate and Zen are really the same.[1]

Of course, what that actually means, or implies, is not at all clear. In fact, it's more like a Zen koan. What is it exactly that somehow manages to turn endless hours of physical training, often exhaustive and filled with aches and pains, into a spiritual endeavor?

I remember once reading an interesting article about this subject—Zen and the martial arts. Some histories make a lot of this connection, and many modern martial arts practitioners would certainly like to believe that there is something more spiritual to their practice, that it's not simply a refined method of brutally dealing with threatening physical attacks. Yet that's exactly the way this commentator put it: that in ancient times, he argued, martial arts was used to kill in life-threatening situations, and that those trained in it—and he applied this also to the samurai—gave little but a passing nod to Zen or any other spiritual concerns. Hence his explanation of why, in many stories, some of these olden-day teachers and martial artists on many occasions did some unsavory things or exhibited less than exemplary morals.

But still, many of us, with fewer battles to fight in modern times, hope that there is a sort of spiritual side to training. As a friend of mine often jokes, "So, after forty years of training martial arts, when do we become enlightened?" Perhaps it's not important, or at least no more important than chasing belt ranks or making it to *shodan*.

Or perhaps we're just not paying attention. After all, there are obvious lessons to be learned: lessons that go beyond learning balance and sensitivity and the fact that sometimes it's important to step back, that one can't always be on the attack. Lessons that go beyond learning fundamental body mechanics through the practice of kata and the realization, after years of training, that all of the techniques are interrelated; that is, they are all connected, just as the body is connected—when one part moves, other parts move as well. These are lessons that spill over from the dojo into other aspects of our lives. And with that, we continue to train ... in

FIGURE 11.1. The entrance to the author's barn dojo

the same way that Kosho Uchiyama Roshi sat Zen: "Sit silently for ten years, then for ten more years, and then for another ten years."[2] But is karate training the same as Zen, as Miyagi said? After all is said and done, are we training karate to reach enlightenment?

I have a close friend I don't see all that often, but we go way back. We've known each other for thirty years or so, and we train together whenever we do manage to get together. We've been to Japan together, and Okinawa, and we've gone on weekends at the Zen monastery. Our interest in Zen Buddhism did not naturally come about because of a shared interest in the martial arts, I don't think, but rather from a similar spiritual interest. We would often have long discussions about books on Zen or how one might reach enlightenment through the practice of the martial arts. These discussions have not been as frequent in recent years, but then, what with family obligations and all, our visits have not been all that frequent either.

Yet every time I see him, he asks me the same question: "So, are you enlightened yet?" We always joke and laugh and leave it at that. Perhaps it's just a conversation starter, much like asking about the weather. Perhaps it's nothing more than a harmless attempt at reestablishing that erstwhile spiritual connection. I wonder what he would think if I said, "Yes, of course"?

I'm not exactly sure what sort of reply one can have to that. Some questions certainly are never meant to be answered. I suppose he would laugh heartily and say, "Oh, come on," as if to imply, "Hey, who are you kidding?" But who's to say? Don't you have to know what enlightenment is yourself to know whether or not someone else has or hasn't reached it? Either that or we're again confounded by our own expectations.

Of course, the connection here for me is when people tell me that *bunkai* can't just be one thing or have one right answer. My response is usually, "Why not? Why can't it?" They suggest that each movement in kata has multiple interpretations or applications. I agree—since I always try to be accommodating—but only *one* of them is correct. What I'm really waiting for is for them to start their response with, "You can't be right because ..." and what follows "because" would be an argument based on the supposition that I have violated logic or clear martial principles, not "because my teacher said so," or "because it's not the *bunkai* we use at our school," or "because it's not what I saw in a book by Master So-and-So," or "because how could you know, you don't even speak Japanese."

When I say that the *bunkai* of the Okinawan classical kata is all about going for the head, I just want someone to *prove* I'm wrong. It shouldn't be terribly difficult to point out where a particular *bunkai* errs. I see it all the time. One of the most egregious errors is when techniques purport to be *bunkai* and then don't follow kata movement. Another is when the attacker seems to be frozen in time, holding his punch out there in midair, allowing the instructor to apply some fancy technique, while out of deference not hitting him in the face with the other hand (the hand that he dutifully holds in chamber). Yet another I often see is when the supposed *bunkai* does not finish the opponent; it looks more as though it would annoy the attacker, rather than make sure that you weren't attacked again by the same person. How logical is it for the creators of kata, whoever they might have been, to have created a system of self-defense where the techniques can have multiple interpretations and *bunkai* can be whatever a fertile imagination can come up with? We need to question things more.

There was a funny political cartoon I saw in the paper. It was by Adam Zyglis. In one panel it showed a guy holding a ruler along the ground— "proof" that the earth was flat. Another panel showed this guy from the seventeenth century pointing at a bird in flight, saying, "If gravity is real, explain that." The last panel showed a dumb looking guy pointing to a snowflake as "proof" that global warming was just a myth concocted by some idiot scientists. It reminded me of the energy we expend trying to protect our turf, trying to safeguard what we think we know, hunkered down behind our own Maginot lines.

Quite a few years ago now, after I had written about Seipai kata in the *Journal of Asian Martial Arts* and how one might look at it based on pretty clearly delineated principles, the article became the subject of a forum discussion for a brief period of time. One person wrote the following: "I am not convinced it is the answer to the kata, if there is one, but it does create a way to hang all the kata together and decipher them with some fairly simple tools." I wondered at the time, what more do you want?

Another said, "It is a good foundation, but I prefer my own methods, although his [mine] are quite interesting.... I do think we will see a lot more of this because so few have a better solution. I think many will copy it. It will become something some 'old man' taught me, or 'something I found' type of thing for many teachers." Yes, perhaps that's the problem; we each prefer our own methods, even if those methods may be illogical.

Another seemed quite receptive until his sensei weighed in on the matter. He said, "When my sensei saw the article, what he questioned the most was, How did the opponent get into the position he was in to begin the technique.... What Sensei questioned in this article was not the technique, but rather, how did he (Giles sensei) get the opponent to enter like that, and what are the chances of being able to reproduce it?" I found this comment the most perplexing. For simplicity's sake, we showed all of the attacks as right or left straight punches. In actuality they could be punches, grabs, or pushes—it doesn't really matter in most cases. In addition, all of it is based on the well-founded Okinawan karate principle that the defender should move in such a way as to allow the attacker only the one initial attack. I even proposed that the kata shows you how to move this way. The techniques all start with the receiving technique (the "block," if you will, though many of the blocks are accompanied by a simultaneous attack). What was this teacher looking at? The attacker got into that position by attacking.

Another critic had a problem with the analysis because, he said, "many of them can't be reasonably practiced safely." That's true, but what does that have to do with whether an analysis is correct or not? The kata is what it is. You don't change the kata because the *bunkai* is too deadly.

Perhaps the most novel criticism of the article came from someone who suggested that I was imposing an "a priori" analysis. He said, "In the beginning, there was only movement. The evil was introduced in this world when the creator wanted to explain them...." But I'm not really sure what that means. In the beginning, I suppose, there was just the random movement of the stars and the planets until someone came up with the idea of gravity. I think he was supposing that I was forcing a theory on the material and then attempting to come up with *bunkai* to justify the theory. Quite the contrary, I think we only formulated the theory or principles after experimenting with *bunkai,* after finding the techniques that were the most effective and made the most sense. It is only then, after working things out on the dojo floor, that one begins to see the principles behind the techniques, and then the principles begin to offer a sort of confirmation for how one is looking at kata. Isn't this something like the scientific method that we all learned in school? That is, we first accumulate data (kata) and then begin to analyze it *(bunkai).* Only after much trial and error (and we are continually revising and refining) do we even begin to formulate theories.

For the life of me, I can't figure out criticism like this. When we feel threatened in any way, the ego runs to our defense. Whatever happened to open and honest discussion?

My teacher, Kimo Wall, to whom I'm greatly indebted for having first set my feet on the path of karate-do, had three sayings that we heard over and over again: "Train hard, train often"; "Open mind, joyful training"; and

FIGURE 11.2. Kimo Wall sensei

"Replace fear and doubt with knowledge and understanding." I'm sure he probably heard them from his teachers. They're certainly worth passing on. But they also need to be a part of one's training ethos. I have tried to keep an open mind and pursue knowledge, sometimes teaching large groups of fifty or sixty students at a time and sometimes training for months at a time with no more than one other senior student. We have trained hard and often, and I'm very thankful for the time I've spent learning from Gibo Seiki sensei and Matayoshi Shinpo sensei. I'm also indebted to Ivan Siff, Bill Diggle, John Jackson, and a host of others, because you can't learn karate without *bunkai,* and you can't do *bunkai* without another person, a kindred spirit. And it is these teachers and fellow students, their friendship and camaraderie in this physical and spiritual endeavor, who have contributed so much to the ideas in this book.

In the meantime, if you ask me if I know the real *bunkai* to the Goju-ryu classical kata, I'll tell you, "Yes, I'm fairly certain about most of the classical kata," but I'm still training and learning. If you ask me how I know, I'll tell you that it conforms to good martial principles, follows the kata exactly, and is realistic. It's also self-referential, as any good system might be. On the other hand, if you ask me whether I've reached enlightenment yet, I'll tell you, "No, not today. Tomorrow, maybe." And then I'll keep training.

It was the end of the summer. The sounds of the market woke us for the last time. We still hadn't gotten used to it. This was not the contemplative silence of a Japan one sees in a Hiroshige print. When we arrived in Okinawa almost two months earlier, we found it to be full of surprises. It had seemed then as if Okinawa had been covered in concrete after the devastation of the Second World War. We had expected something different, but the magic and mystery of Okinawa was still there, just beneath the surface.

We often stopped to visit with Okusan, Matayoshi sensei's wife, before heading off on our explorations, just as we did this morning, our last. She offered us rice balls, and we talked with her as she collected money from the small farmers or gardeners that rented space in the market to sell their produce. Her granddaughter, Nami, played in the back of the office. Some mornings Matayoshi sensei himself would come by and haul us off to visit a famous *Buyo* (dance) teacher or we would all climb into someone's offered van and head off to see the sights of Okinawa.

FIGURE 11.4. Matayoshi with the author's daughter Phoebe

But this morning we were waiting for a van to take us to the airport. To pass the time, Kimo sensei was doing magic tricks for Matayoshi sensei's granddaughter. When he held his hands out, palms up, to show her that they were empty, she looked up with surprise.

"Doko des'ka?" she asked. Where is it? The coin had disappeared.

"I don't know," Kimo sensei said, with feigned innocence. "I've forgotten where I put it. Maybe it's lost." Matayoshi sensei laughed too. He had seen these tricks before. In a minute, the coin would appear again from behind Nami's ear or it would fall from the air as if by magic, our attention on other things.

We look to see what is hidden in the hand, but we don't see it. Sometimes I wonder what else is hidden, what else may have been lost with the deaths of so many of the old masters, lost like Nami's coin, or whether we have simply forgotten where and how to look.

Ganbatte kudasai.

Giles Hopkins
Northampton, Massachusetts
2016

SOME FINAL THOUGHTS AND PRINCIPLES OF KATA ANALYSIS

There are many "principles" one might apply to the study and training of Goju-ryu kata. Some principles have to do with correct martial movement, and many of these principles will hold true across a wide spectrum of martial arts and styles. Other principles, however, have to do with how we can understand a particular martial art and may only apply to how a specific style practices and has preserved the techniques of its system, in this case Goju-ryu. In this appendix, I have listed a number of ideas that I have found useful in analyzing kata. Here is a short list:

- Katas are composed of combinations or sequences of techniques. Certainly there are an almost infinite number of techniques that one can study, but one will never truly understand Goju-ryu as a system until one can clearly see the combinations or sequences contained within the katas.

- There is no first attack in karate—*karate ni sente nashi*. Therefore, in any analysis of kata, it is important to start by looking for the block or receiving technique at the beginning of each combination or sequence of moves. Often these "blocks" are done simultaneously with an attack or "bridging" technique done with the other hand. In any case, the block, together with the controlling or bridging technique, along with proper stepping, should leave the defender in such a position that the attacker does not have a second chance to attack.

- When considering the application or analysis of kata movement, one should keep in mind the principles of stance and weight shifting. Turning, changing directions, and the angles in kata should, at a very basic level, give one an indication of how one might employ the waist, stances, rotation, and body positioning against an opponent. The turns and changes of direction in kata also indicate the direction of attack and how one steps off line. Too often students attempt to analyze the techniques of kata facing each other squarely, as if they were confined to an empty refrigerator box with an opponent.

- To further elaborate on the above point: The stepping—particularly in the initial *uke*—indicates how the defender steps off line and consequently the direction from which the opponent's attack comes. The principle here is that the attacker is attacking one's centerline and the defender is stepping off the centerline to avoid the attack. This is safer and makes blocking easier. In analyzing kata (or looking for *bunkai*), how you step off line with the initial block should show you the direction from which the opponent is attacking. The kata shows these steps and movements in a variety of ways and along various angles. What one sees in kata is a demonstration of how one steps off line. The pattern of kata doesn't show turns because one has run out of space but because it shows both where the attack is coming from and how one should avoid it in applying the technique. What should be apparent then is that in analyzing kata—*bunkai*—one should always start from the end of the previous sequence. And, of course, the lessons one learns here should be applied to other situations, such as *ippon kumite,* where one is facing the attacker.

- Block the hands, protect against an elbow, but attack the head. The attacking techniques of Goju-ryu always seem to go for the head or neck of the opponent. It's generally much deadlier than simple punch-kick responses. Even middle-level punches are often at this level only because the opponent's head has been brought down. Even the *mawashi uke* is generally used as a finishing technique against the opponent's head and neck when we see it in the classical katas of Goju-ryu (Suparinpei, Sanchin, and Tensho being the exceptions).

- Since Goju-ryu is a system of self-defense, when one employs a technique correctly, it should seem effortless. Of course you should put the effort into developing your strength and speed and flexibility, especially when you are young, but the techniques themselves shouldn't depend on strength or speed to work. This is particularly true of the "receiving" techniques of Goju-ryu, which are, for the most part, "soft," generally meeting the opponent's attack with circular blocks that deflect or neutralize the attack. In addition, the position of the arms first encountered in Sanchin training is applied, in principle, to many of the receiving techniques, and when this "immovable arm" is used in conjunction with stepping off line and the rotation of the trunk, any effort or energy the defender uses can be saved for the counterattack, though these counterattacks may be just as effortless if the same understanding of stepping and rotation is used there as well.

- Understanding the structure of a kata is very important. All katas do not conform to the same structure, so this may initially be somewhat confusing and difficult to figure out. But it is important to understand the structure of a kata in order to fully understand the kata and the *bunkai*. In Goju-ryu katas, entry techniques together with their controlling techniques are followed by finishing techniques, but the finishing techniques may sometimes only be shown at the end of the second combination or sequence of repeated techniques. It should also be noted, however, that in some cases the controlling or bridging techniques may be separated from the initial receiving techniques.

- Once you have found the combination or sequence of techniques, the movements within the sequence should be continuous and uninterrupted. No gaps.

- To find and properly understand the techniques, it is important to see how the attacker would respond to each of the defender's techniques. This takes a bit of imagination on the part of both the attacker and the defender studying *bunkai*. So often, because we are either schooled from standing in front of a stationary post or perhaps because we are used to engaging in continuous two-person drills where the agreed-upon idea is not to end the encounter but to continue demonstrating technique, we fail to see how a technique is applied simply because we can't imagine the reaction of the opponent. And the opponent doesn't react to the techniques because the opponent is our dojo training partner and we have "pulled the punches."

- Don't look at the final position—the still photograph of a position one might see in an instructional manual—to explain a technique. The real explanation needs to incorporate the movement of "getting there" from the previous position. For example, the circular block one employs may end up in the *gedan* position, but it may cross one's centerline (what the attacker is attacking) in the upper or middle level. A technique often begins before you think it begins.

- Do the move in *bunkai*, against a partner, exactly how it occurs in kata. This should include any steps or directional changes. If kata is the means that karate teachers chose to preserve and remember technique, then all of the keys for learning how to apply the techniques are in the katas themselves. Nothing is really hidden. It's just that sometimes we don't know what we are looking at.

B

SOME THOUGHTS ON THE PRINCIPLES OF MARTIAL MOVEMENT IN GOJU-RYU

Some principles of martial movement hold true across a wide spectrum of martial arts and styles, particularly Chinese-based systems of self-defense. And though they may not be as readily apparent in karate styles, they are fundamental to the correct practice of Goju-ryu. Here is a short list and brief explanation of some of them:

- "All the joints of the arms should be completely relaxed, with shoulders sunk and elbows folded down."[1] So often, people collect kata or *bunkai* without really learning how to move. Most people who practice karate are far too rigid. It is difficult to learn how to relax. But without relaxation, you won't be fast enough or have real power. If you have never experienced it, then it is also hard to imagine. The joints must be open and relaxed in order to use the whole of the body in each technique. Folding the elbows down— the position of the arms in Sanchin—is one of the lessons we learn from Sanchin kata and one of the lessons we carry over into other katas and many other techniques, in fact almost anytime we "touch arms" with an opponent or do *bunkai*. It is the structural integrity of this position that is so important. If this position is correct, then one is in a position to effectively "block" or withstand the force of the attacker with very little effort.

- "'The Millstone Turns but the Mind Does Not Turn.' The turning of the millstone is a metaphor for the turning of the waist."[2] So often karate students use their arms as if their arms were disconnected from the rest of the body. The arms are moved by the waist. When the waist moves, the arms and legs move. When this is done properly, there is very little effort involved in "blocking" (or receiving) the opponent's attack or in counterattacking. This is difficult to learn from a book or a magazine, and it is especially difficult without first learning how the waist enters into all movement. But once you do see this, then you will see the "hard and soft" in Goju.

- "We avoid the frontal and advance from the side, seizing changing conditions."[3] This is the meaning of the patterns of Goju-ryu kata. We should study all of the turns and direction changes in order to learn how to "avoid the frontal and advance from the side." This is the lesson of the structure and directional changes in Goju kata. So often, students (and teachers) looking to apply the techniques of kata look only at the hands, ignoring the stepping or directional changes of kata. It's as if we're lions caught in a cage at the circus and the only thing we can focus on is the chair held in front of us. The initial movement in kata—the receiving technique in a series—is usually accompanied by the movement, generally off line, of the feet and body. The kata is a teaching device. If you study this one lesson carefully, you will see all sorts of useful things that may not have been apparent before.

- "'Continuity without Interruption.' The power of external stylists is extrinsic and clumsy. Therefore we see it begin and end, continue and break. The old power is exhausted before the new is born.... From beginning to end there is no interruption. Everything is complete and continuous, circular and unending."[4] One should look for this rhythm in kata and *bunkai*. Colloquially, we refer to this principle as "No gaps." So often, students perform kata with a kind of dead, static movement—as if they were demonstrating each position for judges at a tournament or as if they were demonstrating still postures from a book. However, from the beginning of a sequence to the end of that sequence, there should be "continuity without interruption": the movements should be continuous and without gaps. Kata is solo training; it should be practiced as if one were applying the techniques against an opponent. If *bunkai*, by definition, should be done exactly like kata, one might also say that kata should be done exactly like *bunkai*.

- "Never forget for a moment that as soon as one part of the body moves, the whole body moves. Do not move just one part independently."[5] Everything is connected. This is the only way to move effortlessly in a relaxed fashion. It is also the only way to move with real power and speed. So often you see people demonstrate kata without the waist or the legs when they are attacking or blocking with the arms or the hands. It's most notable when people turn in kata to face another direction. They appear to ground themselves firmly in some rigid stance before they attack or block with the hands or arms.

NOTES

INTRODUCTION

1. Patrick McCarthy and Yuriko McCarthy, *Ancient Okinawan Martial Arts, Volume 2: Koryu Uchinadi* (Boston: Tuttle, 1999), 58.
2. Ibid., 51.
3. Ibid., 64.
4. Ibid., 61.
5. Ibid., 65.
6. Ibid.
7. Seikichi Toguchi, *Okinawan Goju-ryu: The Fundamentals of Shorei-kan Karate* (Burbank, CA: Ohara, 1976), 13–14; McCarthy, *Ancient Okinawan Martial Arts*, 48.
8. Dan Smith, "Kata, Bunkai, Tegumi ... (1)," n.d., http://milos.io/kata-bunkai-tegumi-1.
9. Anthony Marquez, "Okinawan Journey: Legacy of the Past," *Bugeisha* 1:1 (1996), 13.
10. Seikichi Toguchi, *Okinawan Goju-ryu II: Advanced Techniques of Shorei-kan Karate* (Burbank, CA: Ohara, 2001), 16.
11. Paul Babladelis, "Interview Meitoku Yagi (Goju Ryu)," 1989. http://tinyurl.com/yalggo26.
12. Lex Opdam, *Karate Goju Ryu Meibukan* (Los Angeles: Empire Books, 2007), 244, 250.
13. Toguchi, *Okinawan Goju-ryu II*, 32.

14. Patrick McCarthy, "Kata: The Enigma of Uchinadi," FightingArts. com, August 26, 2001. http://tinyurl.com/y9qaptyr.

15. Opdam, *Karate*, 244.

16. Christie Nicholson, "We Only Trust Experts If They Agree with Us," *Scientific American*, September 18, 2010. http://tinyurl.com/y9a2cp23.

17. Douglas Wile, *T'ai-Chi Touchstones: Yang Family Secret Transmissions* (New York: Sweet Ch'i Press, 1983), 71.

1. SANCHIN

1. Chojun Miyagi, "Karate-Do Gaisetsu: An Outline of Karate-Do," speech, March 23, 1934, in McCarthy, *Ancient Okinawan Martial Arts*, 23.

2. Steve Cunningham, "Interview with a Fuchow Master," May 31, 1997, http://tinyurl.com/y9php2yx.

3. Genkai Nakaima, "Memories of My Sensei, Chojun Miyagi," trans. Sanzinsoo, Sanzinsoo Okinawa Goju-Ryu Karate-Do, http://yamada-san.blogspot.com. Originally published in *Aoi Umi* 70 (February 1978), 99–100.

2. TENSHO

1. Fred Lohse, "The Matayoshi Family and Kingai-ryu," *Meibukan Magazine* 11 (2009). http://tinyurl.com/yarb7hov.

2. McCarthy, *Ancient Okinawan Martial Arts*, 51.

4. SEIUNCHIN

1. Wile, *T'ai-Chi Touchstones*, 6.

6. SEIPAI

1. Robert Fulghum, *All I Really Need to Know I Learned in Kindergarten: Uncommon Thoughts on Common Things* (New York: Ballantine, 1986), 2–3.

2. Lee Speigel, "Spooky Number Of Americans Believe In Ghosts," Huffington Post, February 2, 2013.

10. SUPARINPEI

1. Personal communication with Fernando Portela Câmara.
2. Fernando Portela Câmara and Mario McKenna, "A Preliminary Analysis of Goju-Ryu Kata Structure," *Journal of Asian Martial Arts* 16:4 (2007), 47–53.

AFTERWORD

1. McCarthy, *Ancient Okinawan Martial Arts*, 50–51.
2. Kosho Uchiyama Roshi, *The Zen Teaching of Homeless Kodo* (Somerville, MA: Wisdom Publications, 2014).

APPENDIX B

1. Yang Ch'eng-fu, quoted in Wile, *T'ai-Chi Touchstones*, 6.
2. Cheng Man-ch'ing, quoted in Wile, *T'ai-Chi Touchstones*, 19.
3. Yang Family Manuscripts, collected by Li Ying-ang, quoted in Wile, *T'ai-Chi Touchstones*, 37.
4. "The Ten Important Points, Oral Instructions of Yang Ch'eng-fu," recorded by Ch'en Wei-ming, quoted in Wile, *T'ai-Chi Touchstones*, 13.
5. Wile, *T'ai-Chi Touchstones*, 113.

BIBLIOGRAPHY

All Gojuryu Network. "Chronology 1900–1949." www.gojuryu.net /viewpage.php?page_id=31.

Babladelis, Paul. "Interview Meitoku Yagi (Goju Ryu)." 1989. http:// tinyurl.com/yalggo26.

Buck, Pearl S. *All Men Are Brothers*. New York: John Day, 1933.

Câmara, Fernando Portela, and Mario McKenna. "A Preliminary Analysis of Goju-Ryu Kata Structure." *Journal of Asian Martial Arts* 16:4 (2007), 47–53.

Cunningham, Steve. "Interview with a Fuchow Master." May 31, 1997. http://tinyurl.com/y9frqd9s.

Flanagan, Richard. *The Narrow Road to the Deep North*. New York: Random House, 2013.

Fulghum, Robert. *All I Really Need to Know I Learned in Kindergarten: Uncommon Thoughts on Common Things*. New York: Ballantine, 1986.

Higaonna, Morio. *Traditional Karate-Do: Okinawa Goju Ryu: The Fundamental Techniques*. Tokyo: Japan Publications, 1985.

Kerr, George H. *Okinawa: The History of an Island People*. Rutland, VT: Tuttle, 1958.

Lohse, Fred. "The Matayoshi Family and Kingai-ryu." *Meibukan Magazine* 11 (2009). http://tinyurl.com/yarb7hov.

Marquez, Anthony. "Okinawan Journey: Legacy of the Past." *Bugeisha* 1:1 (1996), 8-15.

McCarthy, Patrick. "Kata: The Enigma of Uchinadi." FightingArts.com. August 26, 2001. http://tinyurl.com/y9qaptyr.

————. "The Theory and Practice of Tradition Karate." n.d. www.society
.webcentral.com.au/Secrets.htm.

McCarthy, Patrick, and Yuriko McCarthy. *Ancient Okinawan Martial
Arts, Volume 2: Koryu Uchinadi.* Boston: Tuttle, 1999.

Miyagi, Chojun. "Karate-Do Gaisetsu: An Outline of Karate-Do." Speech.
March 23, 1934. In Patrick McCarthy and Yuriko McCarthy, *Ancient
Okinawan Martial Arts, Volume 2: Koryu Uchinadi.* Boston: Tuttle,
1999.

Nakaima, Genkai. "Memories of My Sensei, Chojun Miyagi." Translated by Sanzinsoo, Sanzinsoo Okinawa Goju-Ryu Karate-Do, http://
yamada-san.blogspot.com. Originally published in *Aoi Umi* 70 (February 1978), 99–100.

Nicholson, Christie. "We Only Trust Experts If They Agree with Us." *Scientific American.* September 18, 2010. http://tinyurl.com/y9a2cp23.

Opdam, Lex. *Karate Goju Ryu Meibukan.* Los Angeles: Empire Books,
2007.

Smith, Dan. "Kata, Bunkai, Tegumi … (1)." n.d. http://milos.io/kata-bunkai
-tegumi-1.

————. "Kata, Bunkai, Tegumi … (3)." n.d. http://milos.io/kata-bunkai
-tegumi-3.

————. "Kata, Bunkai, Tegumi … (6)." n.d. http://milos.io/kata-bunkai-
tegumi-6.

Toguchi, Seikichi. *Okinawan Goju-ryu: The Fundamentals of Shorei-kan
Karate.* Burbank, CA: Ohara, 1976.

————. *Okinawan Goju-ryu II: Advanced Techniques of Shorei-kan
Karate.* Burbank, CA: Ohara, 2001.

Uchiyama Roshi, Kosho. *The Zen Teaching of Homeless Kodo.* Somerville, MA: Wisdom Publications, 2014.

Wile, Douglas. *T'ai-Chi Touchstones: Yang Family Secret Transmissions.*
New York: Sweet Ch'i Press, 1983.

INDEX

White Crane. *see also* Kingai-ryu
    fa jing (short power), 14
    Gokenki as teacher of, 10
    Matayoshi and, 162, 190
Wile, Douglas, 223
wrist block, Tensho techniques, 16–18
wrist grab
    defense against cross-hand wrist
      grab, 83
    defense against same-side wrist
      grab, 82
    defense in Sanseiru first sequence,
      128
    response in Saifa first sequence,
      28–31
    response in Seiunchin first
      sequence, 52–57
    response in Seiunchin second
      sequence, 57–61
    Seiunchin and, 50

X

x-block, in Sanseiru, 133–134

Y

Yagi Meitoku, xix
yama uke (mountain block), 71, 168
yielding, blocking (receiving)
    techniques in Goju-ryu, 149
Yue Shi San Shou, 194
yukata, Matayoshi dressed in, 188

Z

zazen, 2
Zen
    karate and, 227–228
    Kosho Uchiyama Roshi and, 229
    story of the closed mind, xxiv
Zen Buddhism, author's interest in,
    229
zenkutsu dachi (front stance), 32

About the Author

GILES HOPKINS has trained in martial arts since 1973, studying a wide range of styles, from Tae Kwon Do and Shotokan karate to White Crane kung fu and Taiji. He is a sixth-degree black belt in Okinawa Goju-ryu and holds a teaching certificate in Matayoshi *kobudo* from the Zen Okinawa Kobudo Renmei. He spent seven years living and training with Kimo Wall, president of Kodokan, in the lineage of Higa Seiko and Matayoshi Shinpo. In the 1980s, he accompanied Wall sensei to Okinawa and trained *kobudo* under Matayoshi, and Goju-ryu under Higa Seikichi and Gibo Seiki of Shodokan. He has written numerous articles on Okinawan karate and *kobudo* for the *Journal of Asian Martial Arts,* among other publications, and blogs at http://goju-ryu.blogspot.com.

A retired English teacher, Hopkins lives in Northampton, Massachusetts, with his wife and three children.

About North Atlantic Books

North Atlantic Books (NAB) is a 501(c)(3) nonprofit publisher committed to a bold exploration of the relationships between mind, body, spirit, culture, and nature. Founded in 1974, NAB aims to nurture a holistic view of the arts, sciences, humanities, and healing. To make a donation or to learn more about our books, authors, events, and newsletter, please visit www.northatlanticbooks.com.